中国科学技术馆

CHINA SCIENCE AND TECHNOLOGY MUSEUM

汉英对照

BE MARCO POLO
FOR ONE DAY

做一天
马可·波罗

发现丝绸之路的智慧

DISCOVER THE WISDOM ALONG THE SILK ROAD

赵洋　主编

张瑶　崔希栋　副主编

北京科学技术出版社

《中国科学技术馆馆史书系》编委会

主编：殷　皓

副主编：苏　青

编委会成员：欧建成　隗京花　庞晓东　廖　红　蒋志明　兰　军　初学基

编辑部主任：齐　欣

编辑部副主任：刘玉花

编辑：谌璐琳　莫小丹　刘　怡

Board of Editors for History Book Series of China Science and Technology Museum

Editor-in-Chief : Yin Hao

Associate Editor-in-Chief : Su Qing

Members of the Board : Ou Jiancheng Wei Jinghua Pang Xiaodong Liao Hong

        Jiang Zhiming Lan Jun Chu Xueji

Head of the Editorial Office : Qi Xin

Assistant Head of the Editorial Office : Liu Yuhua

Editors : Shen Lulin Mo Xiaodan Liu Yi

《做一天马可·波罗：发现丝绸之路的智慧》编委会

"做一天马可·波罗：发现丝绸之路的智慧"展览通过第一人称视角代入的方式，使观众"化身"为古代旅行家，"切身"感受沿陆上丝绸之路和海上丝绸之路传播的古代科技与物质文化，进而体会到古代丝绸之路在实现沿线地区互联互通、经济繁荣、贸易往来、民间交流等方面发挥的作用，并对"一带一路"倡议提出的美好愿景产生向往与憧憬。

700多年前，一位名叫马可·波罗的意大利旅行家踏上了前往神秘东方的漫漫长路。在他之前，已有许多先驱者探索过这条路；在他身后，又有无数后继者拓展着这条路。这条历经千载、绵延万里、横贯亚欧、充满传奇的道路就是举世闻名的丝绸之路。

丝绸是这条道路上最有代表性的商品，除此之外还有香料、宝石、玻璃、瓷器、茶叶等。伴随着贸易往来，不同文明的文化艺术相互交流，科学技术亦不断传播，使丝绸之路不仅仅成为东、西方物品流通的商贸之路、财富之路，更成为各民族人民沟通的智慧之路、友谊之路。

观众徜徉其间，仿佛追随马可·波罗的脚步，重走这条伟大而传奇的道路，感受古丝绸之路为世界带来的沧桑巨变，展望成为"和平之路、繁荣之路、开放之路、创新之路、文明之路"的新丝绸之路的美好前景。

本展览占地面积2000平方米，展品70件（套），分为"对异域的想象""带什么去中国""驿站与驿道""漫游古代中国""海上历险""世界在变"6个展区，图文版和多媒体均为汉英双语，是一个面向国内外观众的"一带一路"专题巡回展览。

Through the first-person perspective, the exhibition themed "Be Marco Polo for One Day: Discover the Wisdom along the Silk Road" makes the visitor "incarnated" as an ancient traveler, feel the ancient science and technology and material culture spread along the Silk Road on Land and Sea, understand the role of the ancient Silk Road in the realization of regional connectivity, economic prosperity, trade complementarity and people-to-people bond, and yearn for and look forward to the good vision written by the Belt and Road Initiative.

More than 700 years ago, an Italian traveler named Marco Polo embarked on a long journey to the mysterious East. Many pioneers had explored this path before him and he was followed by countless others. This road, which has lasted for thousands of years, stretched thousands of miles, spans Europe and Asia, connects the world and is full of legends, is the world-famous Silk Road.

Silk is the most representative commodity on this road, followed by spices, gemstones, glass, porcelain, tea and so on. In the course of trade, the cultures and arts of different civilizations exchanged with each other, and science and technology spread along the road. This made the Silk Road not only a road of commerce and trade for goods between the East and the West and a road of wealth, but also a road of wisdom and friendship for the spiritual communication of different ethnic groups.

The audience seems to follow in the footsteps of Marco Polo, retrace this great and legendary road, feel the great changes brought by the ancient Silk Road to the world, and envision the bright future of the new Silk Road, which is the road to peace, the road to prosperity, the road to openness, the road to innovation and the road to civilization.

This exhibition covers an area of 2000 square meters, with 70 pieces (sets) of exhibits. There are six exhibition areas including "Imagination of Foreign Lands", "Take Commodities to China", "Courier Station and Road", "Wandering around Ancient China", "Maritime Adventure" and "The Changing World". It's pictures, text and multimedia content are displayed in both Chinese and English and it is a "Belt and Road" roving exhibition for the audiences at home and abroad.

目 录
CONTENTS

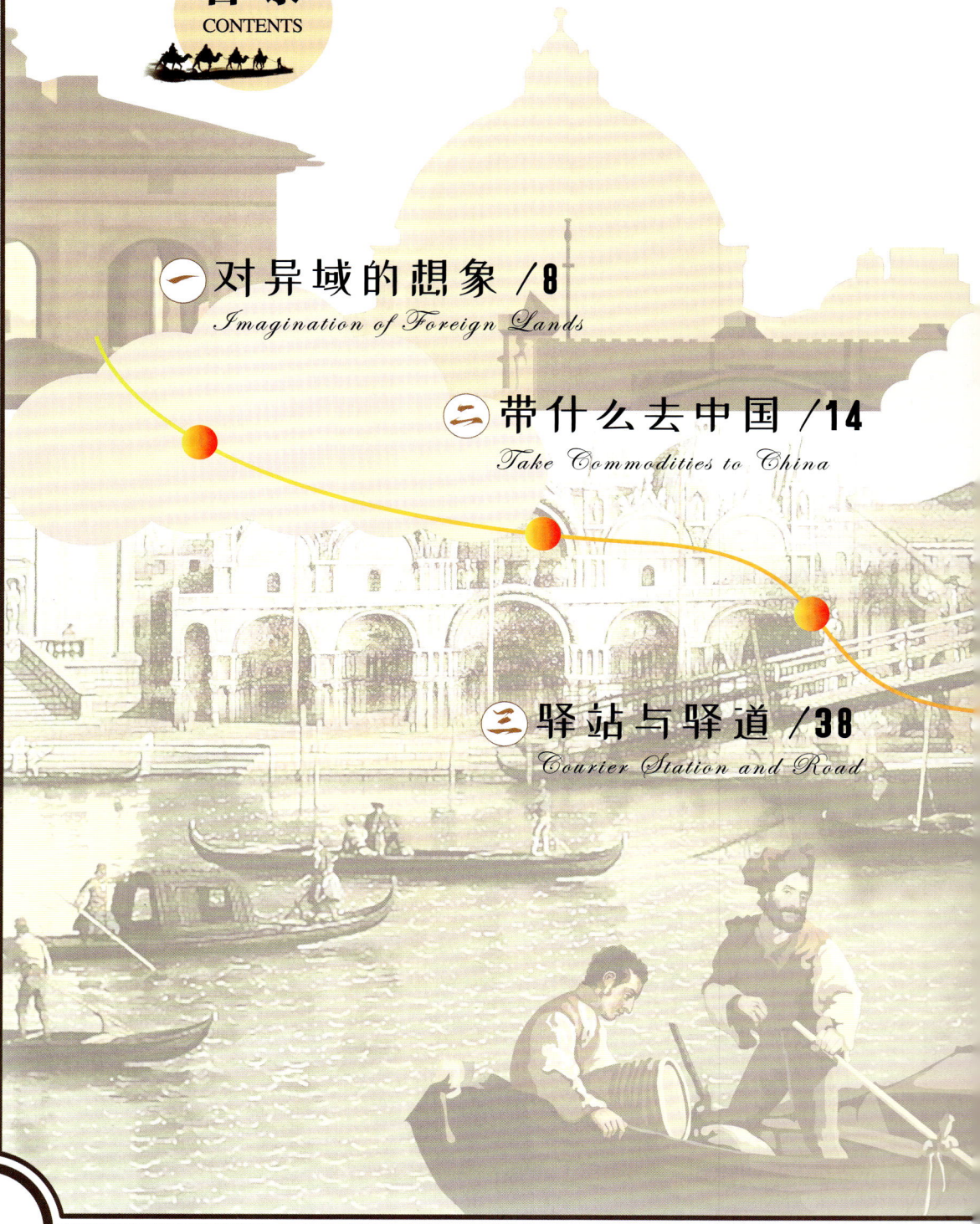

对异域的想象

Imagination of Foreign Lands

当人类还无法靠双脚丈量世界时，东西方的人们从未停止过对异域的想象。 远方的国度是什么样的？ 是否有独特的物产？ 远方的人有着怎样的奇异相貌与生活方式？ 自古以来，欧亚大陆两端的人们一直热切地希望了解对方，并为此做出了种种努力。

"对异域的想象"展区通过展示位于丝绸之路两端的东西方文明对异域的想象，以及"马可·波罗"这一古丝绸之路商旅形象，引导观众了解丝绸之路，以及丝绸之路对古人认知遥远世界的重要性。

When humans could not measure the world by feet, people in the East and the West never stopped imagining the foreign lands. What are the distant countries like? Are there any unique products? What strange looks and lifestyles do people in distant countries have? Since ancient times, people on both sides of the Eurasian continent have been eager to get to know each other and have made various efforts to do so.
The "Imagination of Foreign Lands" exhibition area shows people's imagination to each other in the eastern and western civilizations at both ends of the Silk Road, as well as the image of Marco Polo, an ancient business traveler on the Silk Road, leading the audience to understand the Silk Road and the importance of the Silk Road to ancient people's understanding of the distant world.

1. 丝绸之路上的文明使者：马可·波罗

Civilization Messenger on the Silk Road: Marco Polo

马可·波罗（1254—1324），意大利威尼斯人，世界著名旅行家、商人。

17岁时，马可·波罗跟随父亲和叔叔来到中国，并在中国游历了17年之久。回到威尼斯之后，马可·波罗在一次海战中被俘，在监狱里与小说家鲁斯蒂谦结识。通过马可·波罗的口述，鲁斯蒂谦写成的《马可·波罗游记》记录了这次史诗般的中国之旅。此后的数个世纪里，神奇而富庶的中国成为欧洲人的"欲望发动机"。《马可·波罗游记》直接促进了始于15世纪末的地理大发现，西方地理学家甚至据此绘制了早期的世界地图。目前，《马可·波罗游记》在世界范围内共有各种文字版本达119种之多。

Marco Polo (1254—1324), born on the island of Korčula, raised in Venice, was a famous Italian traveler and businessman.

At the age of 17, Marco Polo travelled after his father Nicolo Polo and his uncle Matteo Polo to China and stayed for 17 years. After returning to Venice, Marco Polo was captured in a naval battle. He met Rustichello da Pisa in prison and, through oral dictation, Rustichello completed *The Travels of Marco Polo*. This book recorded the epic Silk Road tour of Marco Polo. During several centuries after that, the magical and wealthy China became the "desire engine" of Europeans. *The Travels of Marco Polo* directly led to the geographic discovery that began in the late 15th century, and Western geographers even mapped out the early world maps based on this book. At present, *The Travels of Marco Polo* has more than 119 versions in various languages worldwide.

马可·波罗
Marco Polo

2. 对异域的想象
Imagination of Foreign Lands

荷兰代夫特陶瓷工厂生产的瓷匾图
The Porcelain Plaque Produced by the Delft Ceramic Factory in the Netherlands

万水千山或许阻隔了古人探索世界的脚步，但却无法阻碍人们对异域的想象。

在中国，成书于战国时期的《山海经》记载了四海之外大量异类之人及异域之物。书中，身体异形的三首国人、交胫国人、长臂国人，能活800岁的轩辕国人、皮肤异常白皙的白民国人等不胜枚举，此外还有没有嘴巴但不会被饿死的鹱等奇珍异兽，令人叹为观止。

在西方，东方形象不断被书写和改造，时而优美如仙境，时而丑陋如噩梦。自马可·波罗游历亚洲以来，关于东方的想象更成为西方人头脑中挥之不去的奇景。荷兰代夫特陶瓷工厂生产的瓷匾展示了17世纪西方人对中国的想象。

The mountains and rivers may have prevented the ancients from exploring the world, but they cannot hinder their imagination of the foreign land.

In China, *Shan Hai Jing*, written in the Warring States period, records a large number of people from all over the world and things from distant countries and foreign lands. In the book, there are countless strange people with abnormal bodies, such as three-headed people, cross tibial people and long arm people, Xuanyuan people who can live 800 years old, and Bai Guo people with abnormally white skin. Also, there are rare, exotic and breathtaking animals, such as Huan, which have no mouth but will not be starved to death.

In the West, "the image of the East" is continuously written and transformed. Sometimes it is beautiful as a myth and occasionally ugly as a nightmare. Since Marco

《山海经》插图
Illustration in *Shan Hai Jing*

Polo visited Asia, the imagination of the East has become a wonder in the minds of the West. The porcelain plaque produced by the Delft ceramic factory in the Netherlands shows the Western imagination of China in the 17th century.

3. 与马可·波罗同行——数字三维全景地图
Travel with Marco Polo—Digital 3D Panoramic Map

1271—1295年，马可·波罗从意大利威尼斯向东经过地中海、两河流域、伊朗高原、卢特荒漠、帕米尔高原、河西走廊到达元大都；尔后，他又从元大都向南经华北平原、福建泉州至南海海域、马六甲海峡、霍尔木兹，最终回到意大利威尼斯。本数字地图以《马可·波罗游记》记载的路线为基础，涉及沿线28个国家，长4万余千米，面积300万余平方千米，包含4座古代城市复原图、300张历史遗址图片、1000个文化地标及5000余个地图信息点。这是首张对《马可·波罗游记》进行历史注释的交互式数字三维全景地图，观众可以通过肢体动作控制地图选项，"飞越"万水千山与历史名城。

From 1271 to 1295, Marco Polo went from Venice, Italy, to the East: through the Mediterranean Sea, Tigris and Euphrates, the Iranian Plateau, the Lut Desert, across the Pamir Plateau, and the Hexi Corridor to Yuan Dadu; then, from Yuan Dadu to the West: through the North China Plain, to Quanzhou, to the South China Sea, across the Strait of Malacca, to Hormuz, and finally, back to Venice, Italy. Based on the route recorded in *The Travels of Marco Polo*, this digital map covers 28 countries along the route, with a length of more than 40000 kilometers and an area of more than 3 million square kilometers. It includes the simulated restoration images of four ancient cities, 300 pictures of historical sites, 1000 cultural and geographical marks and more than 5000 map information points. This is the first digital interactive, three-dimensional panoramic map with historical annotation on Marco Polo's travels. Visitors can control the map options through body movements and "fly over" thousands of rivers and mountains and historical cities.

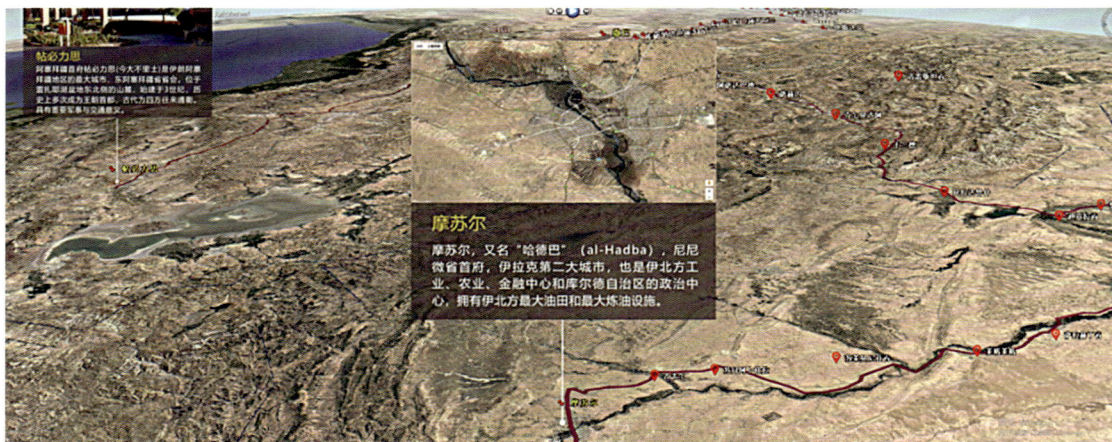

丝绸之路地图
The Map of the Silk Road

科尼亚

科尼亚（Konya），土耳其城市，安纳托利亚高原中南部农业区的主要中心，科尼亚省省会，背靠托罗斯山，面向科尼亚盆地，海拔1027米。

奥特朗托海峡

奥特朗托海峡是地中海中的一个海峡，位于意大利南部与阿尔巴尼亚西部之间，是连接意得里亚海与爱奥尼亚海的重要通道，最窄处75公里，最深处978米。

地图截屏
Screen Capture of the Map

带什么去中国

Take Commodities to China

汉代张骞凿空西域后，中西往来日益频繁。行走在丝绸之路上的西域商人和旅行者会选择携带哪些商品到中国互通有无呢？宝石、水果、香料、药材、玻璃……这些物品承载着西域的技艺与生活方式，丰富了东方的物质与文化。在这个过程中，与贸易有关的数学和度量衡知识也得以交流互鉴。

在"带什么去中国"展区，观众以古代丝路商旅的身份流连于欧洲和西亚、中亚集市，了解西域的水果、宝石、玻璃、药材、香料等知识，并穿插古代丝路贸易用到的数学与度量衡知识，满载异域商品前往中国。

After Zhang Qian's diplomatic mission to the Western Regions in the Han Dynasty, the exchanges between China and the West became increasingly frequent. What goods would the merchants and travelers in the Western Regions on the Silk Road choose to carry to China for exchange? Gemstones, fruits, spices, herbs, glass... These items represented the skills and lifestyles of the Western Regions and enriched the material and culture of the East. In this process, knowledge of trade-related mathematics and weights and measures was also exchanged.

In the exhibition area of "Take Commodities to China", visitors follow in the footprints of merchants along the ancient Silk Road and visit fairs in Europe, West Asia, and Central Asia to learn about fruits, gemstones, glass, herbs, and spices in the Western Regions, and mathematics and measurement knowledge used in the ancient Silk Road trade. With a full load of exotic commodities, they head to China.

1. 这些水果产自哪里
Where Do These Fruits Come From

    丝绸之路的开辟使得沿线国家、地区的商贸和文化交流增多，在互通有无的过程中，原产于中国的梨、枣、桃、李、杏、柿、梅等水果传到世界各地，菠萝、葡萄、西瓜、石榴、椰枣、波罗蜜、无花果等产自西域或东南亚地区的水果也进入了中国。这些水果的引进丰富了中国人的食谱，有一些还作为药材使用，某些水果的种植、栽培技术甚至对中国传统农业技术的发展产生了重要影响。

    The opening up of the Silk Road has increased trade and cultural exchanges among countries and regions along the silk road. In the process of material trading, China's pears, jujubes, peachs, plums, apricots, persimmons, and other fruits are spread all over the world. Meanwhile pineapples, grapes, watermelons, pomegranates, date palms, jackfruits, figs and other fruits from western regions or Southeast Asia have also entered China. The introduction of these fruits has enriched the Chinese diet, some of which are also used as medicinal materials. The planting and cultivation techniques of some fruits even had an important impact on the development of Chinese traditional agricultural technology.

从西域、东南亚等地区传入中国的水果：包括西瓜、甜瓜、无花果、石榴等
Fruits Introduced into China from Western Regions and Southeast Asia : Including watermelon, melon, figs, pomegranates, etc.

2. 宝石颜色的奥秘
Mystery of Precious-Stone Colors

　　各种宝石的化学成分不同，这些成分中的致色元素对光进行了选择性吸收，使宝石具有不同的颜色。例如，红宝石呈现红色是由于红宝石的铬离子选择性吸收了黄绿光和蓝紫光从而透射出橙、红光及部分蓝光。宝石按颜色可以分为无色宝石和彩色宝石两大类。宝石的颜色与透明度、光泽、纯净度等要素共同决定着宝石的价值和视觉效果。

Precious stones have different chemical compositions. The chromogenic elements in these components selectively absorb light, giving gems different colors. For example, a ruby appears red, because its chromiumions absorb yellow-green and blue-purple colors while reflecting orange, red and some blue colors. Precious stones are mainly classified into colorless and colored. gems by color The value and visual effect of a precious stone is determined by its color, transparency, lustre, and clarity.

红宝石原石：红宝石是颜色呈红色的刚玉，红色来自宝石中的铬。作为世界五大名贵宝石之一，它以其颜色鲜红、美艳闻名于世
Raw Gemstone of Ruby : Ruby is red - colored corundum. Red comes from the chromium in the precious stone. As one of the world's top five valuable precious stones, it is known for its bright red color

3. 宝石如何加工
How to Process Precious Stones

西方宝石加工的特点是以彩色宝石为主，与黄金等贵金属搭配，运用了珠宝镶嵌、累丝等工艺。最早的刻面琢型宝石大约出现在公元前2世纪。中世纪时，切割技术和抛光技术进一步发展，产自东南亚的各种宝石运到欧洲后，在当地的宝石加工作坊里进行切割、打磨和抛光。以宗教题材为设计主题的宝石类饰品整体造型繁复奢华、富丽美观。

在中世纪的欧洲，只有贵族才可以佩戴用贵金属和珠宝镶嵌的饰品。同一时期，中国迎来了又一个文明交流的高峰。此时，彩色宝石受到人们的青睐，被广泛用于服装、首饰上。

中国首饰在加工技艺方面吸收了西方的累丝、珐琅彩饰等工艺，并结合了中国传统玉雕技术，且更多地使用彩色宝石作为装饰点缀，种类和形制也更加丰富多样，这些对中国古代首饰发展具有重要意义。

The characteristics of the traditional gemstone processing of the West were mainly based on colored gemstones, matched with precious metals such as gold, and used techniques such as jewelry making, filigree and other techniques. The earliest faceted gemstones appeared in about the 2nd century BC. During the Middle Ages, cutting and polishing techniques were further developed. Gemstones from Southeast Asia were shipped to Europe where they were cut, grinded and polished in local gemstone mills. The gemstone jewelry designed with religious themes were complex and luxurious, rich and beautiful in their overall shape.

In the Middle Ages, only nobles could afford ornaments with precious metals and jewelry. During this period, China ushered in another climax of cultural exchanges. Colored precious stones gained the popularity and were widely used on clothing and jewelry.

The Chinese jewelry integrated Western techniques such as filigree and enamel and with the traditional jade carving technology of China. Colored precious stones were often used for decoration. The variety and shape of jewelry were more diversified. Western processing techniques exerted a significant influence on the development of ancient Chinese jewelry.

拜占庭时期的玉髓浮雕吊坠
Jade Relief Pendant and Brooch，Byzantium

元代的鹘啄鹅绦环
The Gu Jiu Pecks the Swan, Yuan Dynasty

① 《开玉图》
② 《扎碢图》
③ 《冲碢图》
④ 《磨碢图》
⑤ 《掏堂图》
⑥ 《上花图》
⑦ 《打钻图》
⑧ 《透花图》
⑨ 《打眼图》
⑩ 《木碢图》
⑪ 《皮碢图》

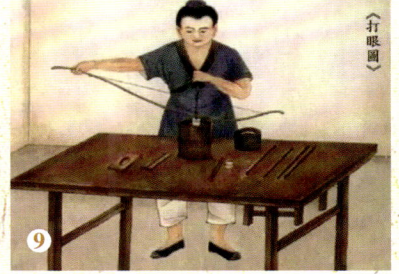

玉石加工过程图
Precious Stone Processing Chart

4. 宝石有多硬
How Hard Can a Precious Stone Be

宝石的硬度指其抵抗外来压力、刻画或研磨等机械作用力的能力，与其化学组成、化学键及晶体结构有关。

宝石硬度的大小是决定宝石耐久性的重要因素，也决定了宝石切割、打磨的难易程度。在史前时期，古人就在玉石加工过程中使用以石英砂为主要材料的"解玉砂"来打磨玉石，所以有"他山之石可以攻玉"的说法。在现代生活中，宝石作为矿物的一部分，除了被当作装饰品外，也广泛用于工业生产过程中，如金刚石作为自然界硬度最高的天然矿物，是优良的研磨材料和切割材料等。

德国矿物学家腓特烈·摩斯根据10种标准矿物的相对硬度确定了10个定性级别，称为摩氏硬度标准（HM）或摩氏硬度计。这10种矿物及其相对硬度分别是滑石1、石膏2、方解石3、萤石4、磷灰石5、正长石6、石英7、黄玉8、刚玉9和金刚石10。

Precious stone hardness stands for its resistance to external forces like pressure, carving, and grinding. The hardness of precious stones is determined by their chemical composition, chemical bond, and crystal structure. Hardness determines the durability of a precious stone, and the difficulty in cutting and polishing. In the prehistoric period, people abraded jade stone with "sand", mainly quartz sand. As the old Chinese saying goes, "The stone of another mountain can abrade jade." In modern times, precious stones are not only used as ornaments, but also applied to industrial production. For instance, diamond, as the hardest natural mineral, is an excellent material for abrading and cutting.

The Mohs scale of mineral hardness was created by German mineralogist Friedrich Mohs, based on the relative hardness of 10 standard minerals. It has 10 qualitative levels, including talc 1, gypsum 2, calcite 3, fluorite 4, apatite 5, orthoclase feldspar 6, quartz 7, topaz 8, corundum 9, and diamond 10.

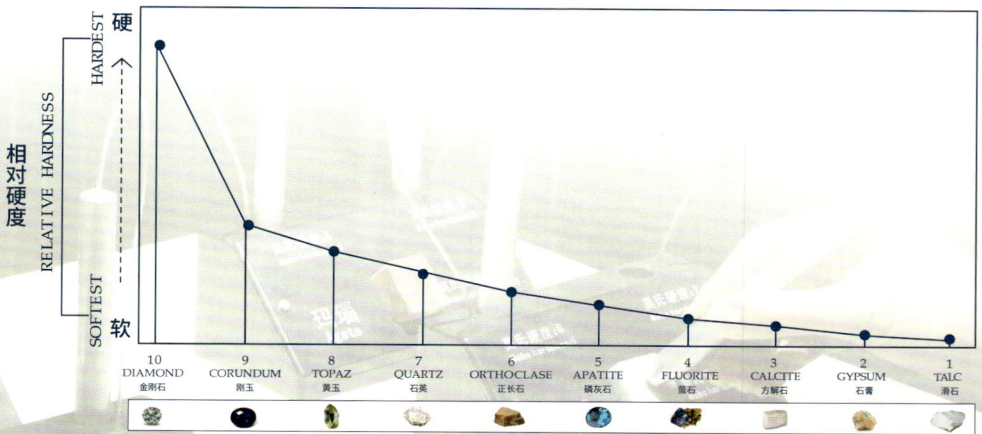

摩氏硬度表
The Mohs Scale of Mineral Hardness

5. 中国古代有玻璃吗
Did Ancient China Make Glass

中国古代是有玻璃的。中国人对玉石的偏爱也使中国古代玻璃器物多是模仿玉器的不透明铅钡玻璃，这与西方流行的钠钙玻璃有明显区别。中国现存最早的玻璃制品出现在春秋时期越王勾践的宝剑上，它的化学成分与古埃及的玻璃不同，制造技术可能是从原始瓷釉技术演变而来的。先秦时期，西方的玻璃已传入中国；魏晋南北朝时期，东西方交流进一步增多，西方玻璃器在中国备受欢迎，埃及玻璃的制造技术也被南方交州、广州一带的工匠所掌握。中国的玻璃制作工艺一直到唐朝中前期都在不断改进发展，直到宋朝，玻璃器的地位才被更符合中国人审美喜好的瓷器所取代。

There was glass in ancient China. As we all know, the Chinese have a profound preference for jade. Therefore by imitating jade, ancient Chinese glassware was mostly opaque lead-barium glass. This was obviously different from the soda-lime glass popular in the West. The earliest extant glassware in China appeared on the sword of Goujian, King of Yue, during the Spring and Autumn period. Its chemical composition is different from that of ancient Egyptian glass. The manufacturing technology may have evolved from the original enamel technology. In the pre-Qin period, western glass had been introduced into China; During the Wei, Jin, Southern and Northern Dynasties, exchanges between the East and the West were further enhanced. Western glassware was very popular in China, and Egyptian glass manufacturing technology was also mastered by craftsmen from Jiaozhou and Guangzhou in the south. China's glass production process has been continuously improved and developed until the middle and early stages of the Tang Dynasty. It was not until the Song Dynasty that the status of glassware was replaced by porcelain, which was more in line with Chinese aesthetic preferences.

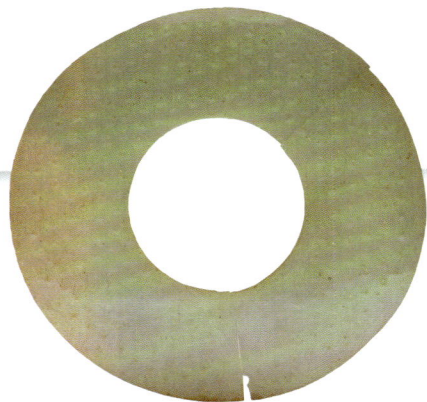

南宋蓝色玻璃双股8节发钗（文物）
Blue Glass Double-Stranded Hairpin with Eight Joints, Southern Song Dynasty (Cultural Relics)

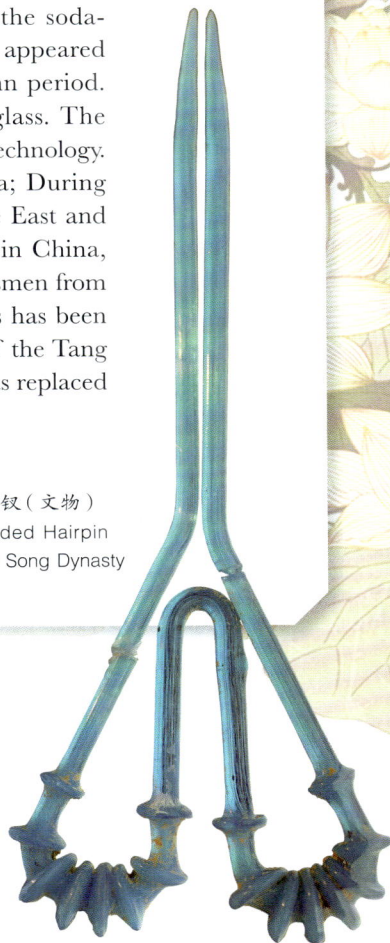

汉代白色玻璃双面乳钉纹璧（文物）
White Glass Double-Sided Nail Patterns，Han Dynasty (Cultural Relics)

6. 来自西方的玻璃

Glass from the West

　　玻璃、陶瓷、青铜是人类最早发明的3种材料，至今还在广泛使用。最古老的玻璃起初是附着在陶珠上，被称为"费昂斯"，出现在公元前3000年前后两河流域的美索不达米亚地区。直到公元前1500年，两河流域才出现真正的玻璃器物。早期玻璃制作工艺有古埃及较为盛行的"型芯法"。公元前4—前1世纪，古罗马人发明了吹制工艺，为玻璃制作技术带来了历史性飞跃。12—15世纪，古代阿拉伯人掌握了玻璃的冷、热加工工艺，使玻璃制品越来越华美。

Glass, ceramics and bronze are the first three materials invented by man and are still widely used today. In around 3000 BC, "Faience", the oldest primitive glass-like material which was originally attached to ceramic beads came into being in Mesopotamia. Not until 1500 BC, real glassware appeared in Mesopotamia. The early glass making process used the "Mold core method" which was more popular in ancient Egypt. Between the 4th century BC and the 1st century BC, the blowing process invented by the ancient Romans catalyzed a technological revolution of glass processing. While in the 12th—15th centuries AD, the cold and hot glass processing techniques mastered by the Arabs resulted in a mature and magnificent decorative style.

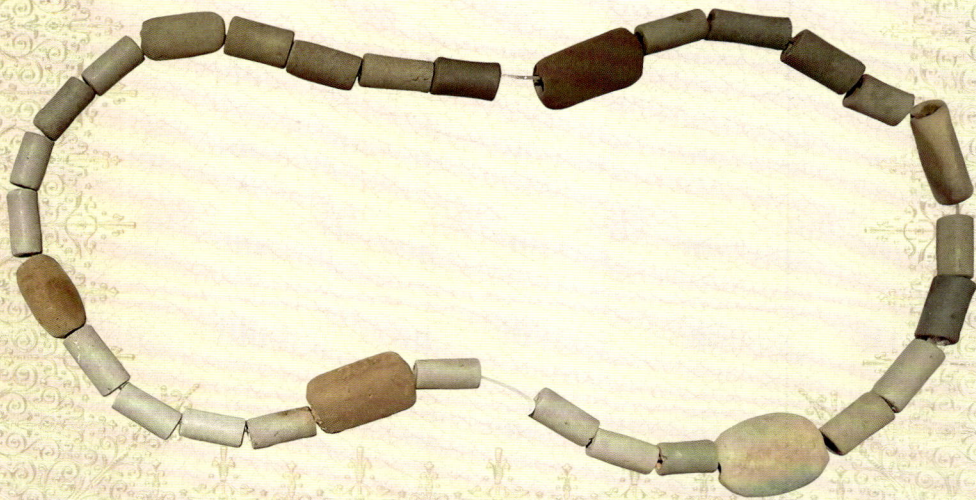

战国时期"费昂斯"串珠（文物）
Warring States Period "Faience" Beading(Cultural Relics)

欧洲古代工艺玻璃器皿（近代仿制品）

Ancient European Craft Glassware(Modern Replica)

7. 如何制造玻璃
How to Make Glass

　　玻璃是用沙子或者石块粉碎后，经高温熔融后形成的一种液态无机物质。由于原料石英砂的化学成分是石英（二氧化硅），它的熔点高达1700℃。古代的烧炉技术难以达到这个温度，所以必须添加助熔剂，将混合物的熔点降低至1000℃以下，才能熔化石英而获得玻璃。助熔剂一般是富含钠、钾成分的天然矿物碱或者草木燃烧之后的灰烬。此外，还需加入一定比例的石灰作为稳定剂，可以保证玻璃的物理结构更加坚固耐久。通过添加不同的着色剂和乳浊剂，可制成模仿天然宝石或者金银效果的彩色玻璃。加入脱色剂后可制成通透似水晶的无色透明玻璃。

Sand or stone is crushed and melted under a high temperature to form a liquid inorganic substance—glass. The chemical composition of raw quartz sand is quartz (silica). The melting point is up to 1700℃. As it was difficult to reach such a high temperature with the ancient techniques, it was necessary to add a flux to drop the melting point of quartz to below 1000℃ to melt quartz into glass. Flux agent is generally a natural mineral base or plant ash rich in sodium and potassium. What's more, quicklime (calcium oxide) is a commonly used stabilizer which can make the physical structure of glass more solid and durable. By adding varied colorants and opacifiers, we could produce colored glass imitating natural gemstones, gold, and silver. While by adding a decolorant, the glass would be as transparent as crystal.

互动游戏"如何制造玻璃"：按下按钮并转动吹管，按照屏幕提示体验制作玻璃器的过程
Interactive Games "How to Make Glass": Press the button and turn the blowpipe, follow the instructions on-screen to experience the process of making glassware

型芯法 MOLD CORE METHOD

在公元前1450—前1100年，古埃及工匠已经可以用型芯制作出色彩缤纷的玻璃器皿，如瓶、罐、盘等。

In 1450–1100BC, ancient Egyptian craftsmen were able to use the mold core method to produce colored glassware, such as bottles, jars, and plates.

制作内芯，用马粪和黏土掺水按一定比例混合，和成泥团；Make the inner core. Mix horse manure, clay, and water to form mud pies;	将一定的泥团包裹铁棍塑成需要的玻璃器形状，并等待干燥；Wrap an iron rod with some mud pies to form the desired shape and let them stand for drying;	将泥团深入熔融玻璃炉中，旋转铁棒，使泥芯表面完全被玻璃包裹；Insert the mud pies into the furnace and rotate the iron rod till the core is completely covered by glass;	器物表面彩色装饰加工；Coloring and decoration;	玻璃器退火后，移除铁棍和内核陶土；After the glass is annealed, remove the iron rod and the core clay;	完成玻璃瓶制作。The glass bottle is completed.
第1步	第2步	第3步	第4步	第5步	第6步

吹制法 BLOWING METHOD

公元前1世纪古罗马帝国时期出现的"吹制法"是玻璃制作史上的第一次重大技术革新，从此玻璃的成型工艺被简化，产量有很大提升。玻璃器的优美造型、流畅线条和匀称器壁都应归功于先进的吹制技术。

Blowing method: The "blowing method" appeared in ancient Rome in the 1st century BC. It marked the first major technological innovation in the history of glass production. Since then, glass molding was simplified. And the output of glassware was improved a lot. Thanks to the blowing method, glassware had beautiful shapes, smooth lines, and even walls.

古代玻璃的塑形工艺
Ancient Glass Molding

8. 认识西域药材
Knowledge about Western Medicine

中国早在汉代便有引进西域药物的记载。中国最早的药学著作《神农本草经》中就收录了菌桂、胡麻、犀角、戎盐等数种外来药。

南朝时期，军队中用从西域传入的琥珀为士兵治疗外伤，疗效显著。

随着中西贸易往来增多，引入中国的西域药材种类也更加丰富，如苜蓿、没药、阿魏、没石子、硇砂、鍮石、黄丹等，逐步丰富了中国的药用资源与临床用药经验。唐代时，绿盐传入中原地区，《海药本草》指出了绿盐可治疗眼疾。

西域药材的不断引进，促进了中西各国医药学的交流，推动了中医药的蓬勃发展。

The introduction of western medicine had been recorded in China as early as the Han Dynasty. The earliest pharmaceutical work in China, *Sheng Nong's Herbal Classic*, included several foreign medicines, such as cinnamon, flax, rhinoceros horn and halitum.

In the Southern Dynasty, amber introduced from the Western Regions was used by the army to treat soldiers' injuries.

With the increasing trade between China and the West, there was the continuous introduction of western medicine, such as alfalfa, myrrh, Ferula asafetida, Aleppo gall, sal ammoniac, calamine and yellow lead. The Chinese medicine resources and clinical medication experience enriched a lot. During the Tang Dynasty, green salts were introduced into the Central Plains. *Herbal Foundation of Overseas Medicines* points out that green salts can cure eye diseases.

The continuous introduction of western medicine has promoted the medical exchanges between Chinese and Western countries and lead the vigorous development of Chinese medicine.

植物形态
Plant form

成药形态
Medicine form

阿魏：一种多年生草本植物，主要分布在西亚、中亚、南亚、南欧及北非部分地区，其根部厚实多肉，内部树脂可入药，可治疗心腹冷痛、疟疾、痢疾、风湿、关节疼痛等。阿魏大约在隋朝时经中亚地区传入中国

Asafoetida : A perennial herb,mainly distributed in Western Asia, Central Asia, South Asia, Southern Europe and North Africa. Its root is thick and fleshy. The latex extracted from the root can be used as medicine to treat cold pain in the heart and abdomen, malaria, dysentery, rheumatism, and joint pain. It was introduced to China through Central Asia during the Sui Dynasty

成药形态
Medicine form

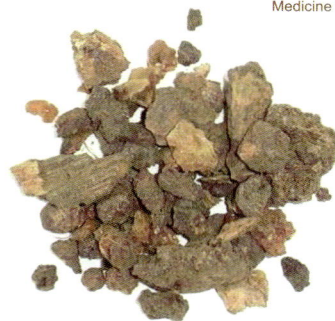

成药形态
Medicine form

绿盐：一种绿色结晶状的硫酸铜矿物。在世界各地均有储藏，以伊朗和中亚地区出产的为最优。绿盐磨碎之后作为外用药点入眼中可以治疗眼科白翳病

Green Salt : A kind of green crystalline copper sulfate ore. There are reserves all over the world, but the green salts produced in Iran and Central Asia are of the highest quality. Green salts can be used as an external medication point to treat ophthalmic white panicle after grinding

没药：没药树分泌的树脂。有活血、消肿、散淤、止痛等作用。原产于西亚、东非，隋朝时传入中国

Myrrh : As the resin secreted by myrrh tree, myrrh has the function of promoting blood circulation, reducing swelling, dispersing stasis and relieving pain. Originating in West Asia and East Africa, it was introduced into China during the Sui Dynasty

9. 古代西方药材加工工具
Western Medicine Processing Tools in the Ancient Times

古代西方的药材加工工具主要有以下几种：

研钵是用于盛放和研碎药用植物的容器，一般用石质材料制成，又称药臼。

药杵是用于研碎药用植物的棒状器具，一般用石质材料制成，与研钵一起配合使用。

漏斗是底部开有小孔的筒型物体，在制药过程中将研碎的药材放入其中，下方摆放器皿收集从其小孔处渗漏下来的药材汁液等物质。

药盆是用于收集药材的器皿。

取脂器是通过挤压方式提取植物药材中树脂的器具。

药瓶是用于盛放成药的容器，一般采用陶制、玻璃材质和金属材质。

天平是用于称量药材的工具。

In the ancient times, there were several western medicine processing tools as listed below.

Mortar: It is a container for crushing medicinal plants, usually made of stone.

Medicine Pestle: As a tool for grinding medicinal plants, it was usually made of stone materials and used together with a mortar.

Funnel: It is a cylinder-shaped object with a small hole at the bottom, into which the ground medicine is put while processing and a vessel is placed below to collect the medicine juice and other substances leaked from the hole.

Medicine Basin: A vessel used to collect medicinal materials.

Resin Extractor: It is an apparatus for extracting resin from plant medicinal materials by extrusion.

Medicine Bottle: It is a container for holding patent medicine, usually made of ceramic, glass or metal.

Balance: A tool for weighing medicinal materials.

取脂器（仿制品）
Resin Extractor（Replica）

研钵与药杵（仿制品）
Mortar and Medicine Pestle（Replica）

漏斗（仿制品）
Funnel（Replica）

10. 香料的加工
Processing of Spices

对于中世纪的欧洲来说，远东和东南亚盛产的香料既可以给食品增添浓烈的香味，又可以作为供奉神灵的圣物，还可以作为养生治病的灵药。欧洲的气候条件不适宜大规模种植香料植物，因此大宗香料主要由商人经海路输往西方。传统香料加工工艺包括风干法、研磨法、蒸馏法等。风干法一般用于加工需要保持外形完整的香料，这些香料包括胡椒、桂皮、丁香、姜、肉豆蔻等用于烹饪的香料。研磨法可用于加工植物的花朵、叶片或混合型香料。蒸馏法用于提取传统精油和纯露水。

For Europe in the Middle Ages, the spices abounded in the Far East and Southeast Asia could not only add a strong fragrance to food but also serve as holy offerings to gods, as well as a magic medicine for health and cure. European climate conditions were not suitable for large-scale cultivation of spice plants, thus bulk spices were mainly exported to the West by sea from merchants. Traditional spice processing methods can be classified into drying, grinding, and distillation, etc. The air-drying method is generally used to process spices that need to be kept in shapes, such as pepper, cinnamon, cloves, ginger, nutmeg and other spices used in cooking. The grinding method can be used to process flowers, leaves or mixed spices. The distillation method is used to extract traditional essential oils and hydrolats.

蒸馏器：将采集的鲜花洗净后放置于蒸馏器里面进行烧制，同时将蒸汽引入冷却器中，待完全冷却后，冷却器中的上层即为精油，下层为纯露水

Distillator : Freshly picked flowers are washed and placed in a special distiller for hesting. At the same time, steam is introduced into the cooler. After completely cooling, the upper layer in the cooler will be essential oil, while the lower layer, hydrolate

11. 你认识这些香料吗
Do You Know These Spices

藏红花 / Saffron

原产于希腊，是一种名贵的香料和药材，由番红花的花朵柱头经过烘干后制成，可作为食品调味剂与着色剂。

Saffron is a rare spice, native to Greece. Made from dried flower stigmas of crocuses, saffron is used as a food flavouring and colourant.

肉豆蔻 / Nutmeg

原产于印度尼西亚、马来西亚。种子可外用驱蚊或用于烹饪，但多食会中毒。

Nutmeg is native to Indonesia and Malaysia. The seeds can be used for de-worming treatment and cooking. People can be poisoned by overeating it.

檀香 / Sandalwood

檀香树原产于印度，树干、树枝具有强烈的香气，也可用于提取精油，是名贵的香料与药材。

The sandalwood tree is native to India. Its trunk and branches have a strong aroma. As a valuable spice and medicinal material, it can also be used to extract essential oils.

肉桂 / Cinnamon

　　肉桂树主要分布在印度、中国及东南亚部分地区，树皮可被制成香料，用于各类烹饪。

Cinnamon trees are mainly distributed in India, China and parts of Southeast Asia. The bark can be made into spices for various cooking.

苏合香 / Styrax

　　苏合香树主要分布在土耳其西南部及希腊罗德岛，所分泌的树脂可加工制成苏合香，常用于制作香囊。

Styrax trees are mainly distributed in southwestern Turkey and Rhodes Island, Greece. The resin secreted can be processed into Styrax, which is often used to make sachets.

胡椒 / Pepper

　　原产于印度。胡椒果实可用于调味以增加食欲，亦可作为胃寒药。

Native to India, the fruit of pepper could be used as a condiment to increase appetite and as a remedy for the stomach cold.

孜然 / Cumin

　　原产于埃及、埃塞俄比亚，果实富含精油，烘干后可用于调味，也可入药。

Cumin is native to Egypt and Ethiopia. The fruit is rich in essential oils and can be dried for seasoning or medicine.

乳香 / Frankincense

　　原产于阿拉伯半岛，由乳香树树皮分泌的树脂制成，可用于制作精油或药膏。

Frankincense is native to the Arabian Peninsula and is made of resin secreted from the bark of the Boswellia tree. It can be used to make essential oils or ointments.

12. 计算工具
Calculation Tools

　　人类历史上先后出现了多种不同形态的计算工具，无论其功能多么强大，实质都是将本应由人脑承担的部分脑力劳动转由计算工具来承担，其算法本质仍然是基于记数法的数字间加减乘除等计算，只不过这些算法被转移到了口诀、算表和计算工具的内部。中国算盘是中国古代传统的计算工具，而在古罗马时期同样出现了被称为古罗马沟算盘的计算工具。二者在结构外形、示数方式、计算原理上都各有特色。除此之外，还有沙盘和算板等计算工具。

A variety of calculation tools of different forms appeared successively in human history. No matter how powerful they may be, the essence is to transfer some of the mental work that should be done by the human brain to the calculation tools. The essence of the algorithm is still based on the arithmetic of adding, subtracting, multiplying and dividing numbers. However, these algorithms have been transferred to formulas, tables, and calculation tools. The Chinese abacus, a traditional calculation tool, was commonly used in ancient China, while in ancient Rome, the hand abacus was used for calculation. They have different structures, appearances, methods of number demonstration and calculation principles. Apart from that, there are other calculation tools such as the sand table and the counting board.

罗马沟算盘：只有手掌大小，用金属制造，有小珠嵌在上下两排沟槽中，可以滑动但不能取走
Roman Abacus with Embedded Beans : It was as small as the palm, made of metal. This abacus used beads on two rows of wires. The beads could be moved rather than removed

中国串珠算盘：起初为一四算盘，每档能表示0到9的数字，到明代时改革成二五算盘，每档能表示0到15的数字，成为一种16进制和10进制通用的计算工具
The Chinese Abacus : The Chinese abacus was originally a one-four abacus, each of which could represent the numbers from 0 to 9. While in the Ming Dynasty, the abacus was reformed into a two-five abacus, each of which could represent the numbers from 0 to 15. Hereby it became a universal computing tool for hexadecimal and decimal number systems

沙盘、算板：沙盘是指在平板上铺上细沙，用来写字和计算；算板是在木板或石板上刻上若干平行的线纹，上面放卵石来记数和计算

Sand Table and Counting Board : A sand table uses constrained sand for writing and calculation. A counting board was made of wood or marble. Parallel lines were carved on it. Pebbles were put on it for counting and calculation

13. 九九乘法与格子算法
The Jiujiu Multiplication Table and the Grid Multiplication Chart

当记数法出现后，随着问题的复杂化和运算数字的增大，逐渐演化出与相关记数法相匹配的运算法则。

中国古代很早便利用"九九乘法口诀"来解决实际应用中的乘法运算，出土于湖南省的里耶秦简是现已发现最早记录"九九乘法口诀"的出土文物。2000多年来，乘法口诀一直都是中国人进行乘法计算的重要工具。13—15世纪阿拉伯数学家提出了一种"格子算法"，用以解决多位数相乘的运算，后来这种算法传入欧洲和中国等地。中国明代的多本数学著作也记载了这一算法，称为"写算"或"铺地锦"。

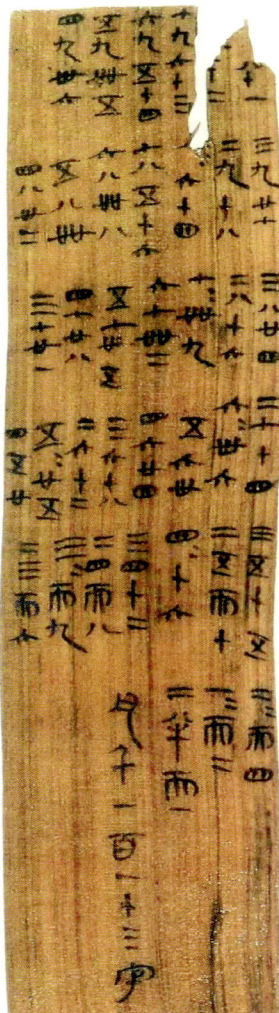

After the numeral system was proposed, as problems became more complicated and the numbers increased, rules of arithmetic corresponding to the numeral system gradually developed.

The "Jiujiu multiplication table" had long been used in ancient China to solve practical multiplication arithmetic. The Liye Qin Slipe, unearthed in Hunan Province, is the earliest unearthed document that records the "Jiujiu multiplication table". For more than two thousand years, the "Jiujiu multiplication table" has always been an important tool for the Chinese to perform multiplication calculations. Between the 13th and the 15th centuries, Arabic mathematicians put forward a "grid multiplication chart" to solve the multi-digit multiplication arithmetic. Later, it was introduced into Europe and China, etc. This calculation method was also recorded in many mathematical works of the Ming Dynasty, known as "writing calculation" or "paved brocade calculation".

里耶秦简（公元前3世纪）中的"九九乘法口诀"
The "Jiujiu Multiplication Table" in the Liye Qin Slipe (3rd Century BC)

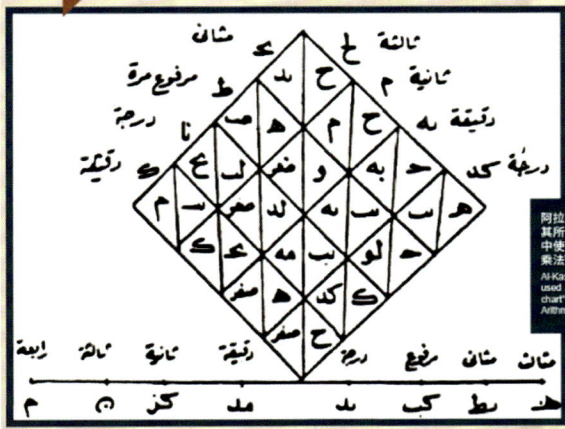

印度—阿拉伯数学中的"格子乘法"
The "Grid Multiplication" in the Hindu-Arabic Mathematics

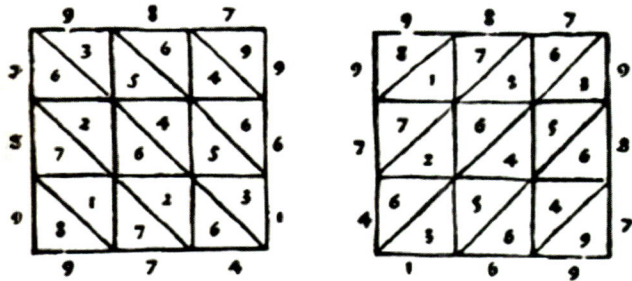

欧洲数学中的"格子乘法"
The "Grid Multiplication" in the European Mathematics

中国数学中的"铺地锦"
"Paved Brocade Calculation" in the Chinese Mathematics

14. 3 种记数法
Three Kinds of Notation

记数法是记录或标记数目的方法，是算数运算的基础，主要指数字符号表现形态和计数工具的使用。受自然环境与社会条件的影响，各地产生出不同的计数法。中国古代采用十进位制的算筹记数法。罗马记数法通行于古罗马，是欧洲在印度—阿拉伯数字传入前使用的记数法。印度—阿拉伯数字是由古印度人发明、经阿拉伯人向外传播的，因其笔画简单、结构科学、形象清晰、组数简短等特点而在世界各国通行。

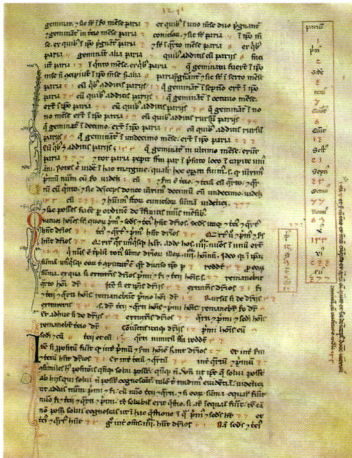

阿拉伯数字进入欧洲
Arabic Numerals Spreaded to Europe

The Notation is a method which records or symbolizes numbers. As the foundation of mathematical calculation, it refers mainly to the manifestation of digital symbols and the use of notation tools. Influenced by the natural environment and social circumstances, people in different regions have developed different types of notation. A decimal system of rod numerals was adopted in ancient China while the Roman numeral system was widely used in Rome and Europe. The latter gave place to the Arabic numeral system upon its introduction into Europe. Hindu-Arabic numerals were invented by ancient Indians and spread to the outside world by Arabs. Due to the features of few strokes, scientific structures, clear images, and short combination of numbers, etc., the use of Arabic numerals became widespread in many countries.

印度—阿拉伯数字符号的演化
The Evolution of Hindu-Arabic Numeral Symbols

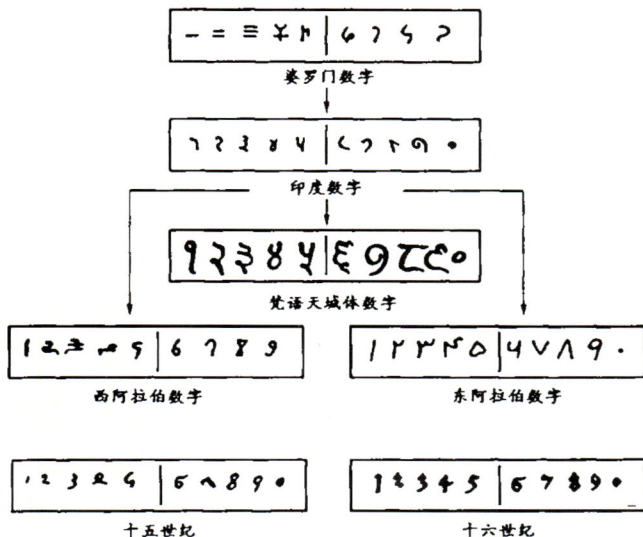

15. 东西方的秤
Scales of the East and the West

　　人类从制造最简单的工具开始就产生了量的概念，也开始了测量活动。中国古代称这种测量为度量衡，衡是关于轻重的量。衡具在丝路贸易中发挥着重要作用，较为常用的一种衡具是杆秤。各国的杆秤样式虽有不同，但都是利用杠杆平衡原理称重量。中国杆秤至少已有千年的历史，还逐渐制定了规章制度以保证重量单位的统一。元代，为了适应外国人到中国经商的需要，还在秤锤上铸（刻）不同的民族文字。同时期欧洲的度量衡并不统一，不同地区1盎司的重量就各不相同。

After inventing the simplest tools, humans had the concept of quantity and started measuring. In ancient China, measurement included length (du), capacity (liang), and weight (heng). Weights and measures played an essential role in the Silk Road trade. One of the more commonly used weights and measures was the steelyard. Although there are different styles of steelyard in different countries, they all use the lever balance principle to weigh the weight. To Chinese steelyard has a history of at least a thousand years and China has gradually developed rules and regulations to ensure the unity of weight units. For the convenience of foreign businessmen in China, the Yuan government even carved different national characters on the sliding weight. During this period, the weights and measures of Europe were not unified. The weight of one ounce in different regions was different.

元代铜权复制品
Bronze Weight, Yuan Dynasty
（Replica）

中国近代木铁质杆秤
Wood Iron Steelyard , Modern China

18世末19世纪初的欧洲秤
European Scale, Late 18th to Early
19th Century

中国清代戥子秤
Dengzi Scale, Qing Dynasty

三

驿站与驿道

Courier Station and Road

在漫长的陆上丝绸之路上，驿站星罗棋布。它们是一个个交通节点，人员和物资通过这些节点在遍布大地的路网上往来穿梭。发达的道路基础设施、高效的信息传递方式、多样化的交通工具、旅途中的食物与用具……共同构成了古典全球化时代的交通情景。

在"驿站与驿道"展区，观众或"行走"于丝绸之路上的驿道和桥梁，或"小憩"于驿站之中，在感受元代邮驿系统高效和快捷的同时，了解古代丝路商旅使用的装备，以及马具、饮食、桌椅、乐器等沿丝路的传播与演变。

The long Silk Road was dotted with post stations. They are traffic nodes through which people and goods travel across the network of roads. Developed road infrastructure, efficient means of information transmission, diversified means of transportation, food and utensils in the journey constituted the transportation landscape in the era of classical globalization.

In the exhibition area of "Courier Station and Road", visitors can "pass" by the post roads and bridges along the Silk Road or "take a rest" at the post stations. While experiencing the efficient and convenient post system of the Yuan Dynasty, visitors can learn about the communication and evolution of the gear and horse harness, food, tables and chairs, and musical instruments used by the merchants.

1. 丝路商旅随身带什么
What Did the Travelling Merchants Take with Them on the Silk Road

俗语说"在家千日好，出门万事难"。古人不像今人能来场"说走就走的旅行"，必须提前备好各类旅途物资，才能放心地踏出第一步。陆上丝绸之路的古代商旅都会携带必要食材和生活物资。

As the saying goes, "It's easy to stay at home a year and it's hard to go out an hour." Ancient people could not have a trip without a plan. They must prepare the traveling bag in advance, before taking the first step assuredly. Travelers crossing the land Silk Road Would bring the necessary food and living materials.

吉布尼奶酪 / Cheese

最初由阿拉伯半岛的贝都因人用山羊奶或绵羊奶制成，是中东地区的人广泛食用的一种白色软奶酪。

Originally, it was made from goat or sheep milk by the Bedouins in the Arabian Peninsula. It was a white soft cheese widely eaten by people in the Middle East.

酸奶汤 / Yoghurt Soup

源于伊朗西北部和阿塞拜疆，盛行于中东地区，由酸奶、菜叶添加香料后煮成。

Originated from northwest Iran and Azerbaijan, popular in the Middle East, it is made with spices, yoghurt, and vegetables.

馕 / Nang

起源于波斯的发酵面饼，是西亚、中亚和南亚许多民族，以及中国西部一些民族的主食。它不易变质，常作为干粮携带。

It was a fermented bread that originated in Persia. It is a staple of many ethnic groups in West Asia, Central Asia, South Asia, and West China. It is less likely to deteriorate, so it is often taken by people as solid food.

肉干 / Dried Meat

人们将肉切成片状或条状，使用盐腌、烟熏等方法加工为肉干，既可以改善风味，也能延长存放时间。

Meat was chopped or cut into strips. It was salted or smoked to improve the taste and prolong the storage time.

水壶 / Kettle

如果商队要穿越沙漠，事先需要储备多日的饮水。个人则会携带皮革做的水壶来盛放饮水。

If it wanted to cross the desert, the caravan needed to have water enough for a few days. Travelers would take a leather bag along with them to store water.

帐篷 / Tent

只有商队的核心人物可以在帐篷内休息，宿营时大部分旅行者只能在牲畜群中坐卧，这些动物可以帮助他们抵挡风沙。

Only the core members of the caravan could rest in a tent during camping. Most travelers could only sit or lie down in the herd overnight. The animals could help resist wind and sand.

毡毯 / Felt Carpet

用毛毡制成的毯子，方便人们在旅途中席地坐卧，使休息变得更舒适。

Travelers could rest comfortably and pray on a felt carpet.

象棋 / Chess

旅行者携带的娱乐用品，起源于古印度，随后向东西方传播。

For entertainment. Chess originated in ancient India and was spread to the East and the West.

2. 驼具
Camel Harness

　　丝绸之路跨越了很多干旱少水的地区，骆驼是那里最重要的运输工具。尽管它们的速度不快，但很适合在恶劣条件下长途跋涉，而且力气大，可以负载约300千克的重物。古代商队常把多达150头骆驼用绳子连成队列，非常壮观。驼具是驾驭骆驼所需要的一套装备，包括驼衣、笼头、驼绳、驼鞍、驼绊、驼镫、驼鞭、驼铃和驼毛收集工具等。

The Silk Road spanned many arid areas. Camels were the most important means of transportation. Although they are not fast, camels adapt to the harsh conditions during the long travels. And a camel can carry approximately 300kg. The ancient caravan used to tie up to 150 camels to form a camel string. It was a grand sight. Camel harness is a set of equipment to saddle camels, including fabric, halter, rein, saddle, lock, stirrup, whip, bell, and camel hair collector.

驼鞍 / Saddle

　　主要结构是前后相连的两个"人"字形的木架，位于驼峰之间，架上可以放置坐垫以供人乘坐。

The saddle is comprised of two upside-down, Y-shaped pieces of wood that are placed between the humps. People sit on a cushion atop the wooden framework.

驼鞍垫 / Saddle Pad

　　垫在驼鞍之下，一般用毯子或毡子制成，主要作用是护驼背、当衬垫，亦作为装饰。

It is the main part of the saddle. Usually, it is made of a blanket or a rug. It can protect the camel's back, and it can be used as a pad or for decoration.

骆驼跪垫 / Hassock for the Camel

　　通常用皮革或毡毯制成，供骆驼在砾石地面跪卧时使用，避免膝部磨损。

It is usually made of leather or blankets. When a camel kneels or lies down, it is used to prevent abrasion.

骆驼鼻棍 / Nose Stick

穿过骆驼鼻部，连接缰绳，用于控制和指挥骆驼。

It is fastened through the camel's nose and connected to the rein. It is used to control and direct the camel.

骆驼笼头 / Halter

可以系上缰绳以便牵引或者拴住骆驼，可分为公驼笼头、驼羔笼头、骑驼笼头等。

It can be attached to the rein to pull or tie the camel. Halters are classified into the halter for a male camel, the haler for a baby camel, the halter for a camel for riding.

缰绳 / Rein

是一条直径约2.5厘米的驼毛绳，一头拴在骆驼鼻棍上，一头由牧人掌握。

It is a rope made of camel hair about 2.5cm in diameter. One end is attached to the nose stick, while the other end is held by the herdsman.

驼铃 / Bell

主要由一列驼队中的尾驼佩戴，行走时发出叮当响声，起提示预警作用。

Usually, the last camel of a caravan wears a bell. When it walks, the bell rings as a warning.

驼镫 / Stirrup

借鉴马镫设计的驼镫，帮助骑乘。

A stirrup makes it easy to mount a camel.

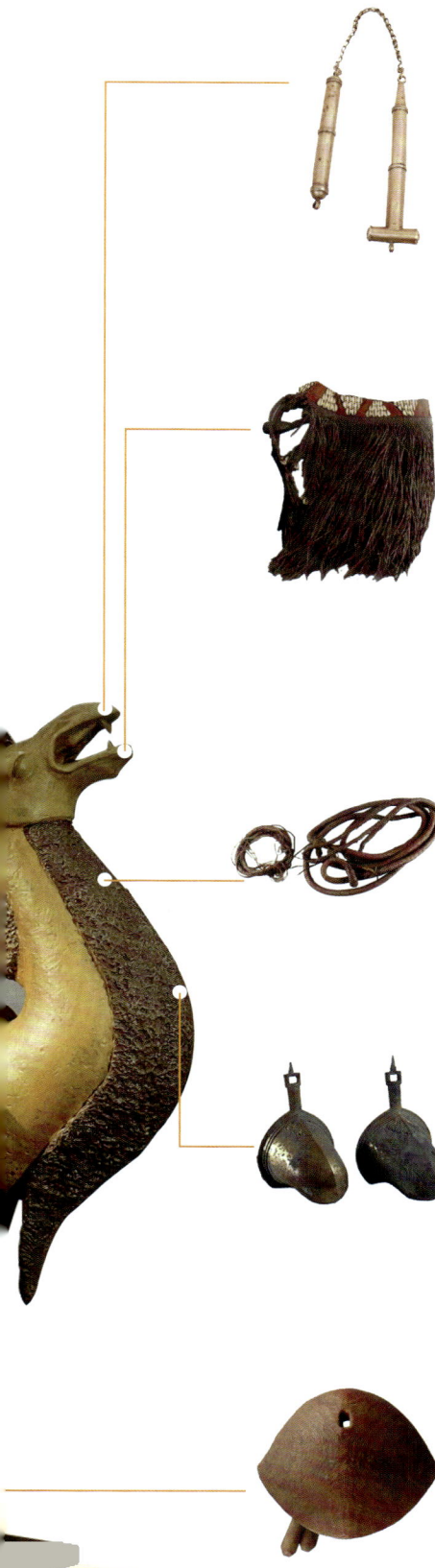

3. 马镫
Stirrup

　　马镫是一件看似很小但作用巨大的发明。它不仅能帮助人上马，更主要是用于骑手在马上支撑双脚，起稳定身体的作用，从而使骑手的双手更加自由。汉代末年，最早的马镫出现在蒙古高原及周边地区，随后传入中原地带和朝鲜半岛。随着突厥人和波斯帝国、东罗马帝国的交往，以及数百年间的民族迁移，马镫逐渐传入西亚和欧洲，最终促进了欧洲中世纪骑士阶层的兴起。

The stirrup is a metal ring that hangs beneath the saddle for people to mount and pedal as they ride. It not only helps people mount the horse, but also support the rider's feet when riding. Thus, the rider can balance the body and free the hands. In the late Han Dynasty, the earliest stirrup appeared in the Mongolian Plateau and surrounding areas, then spread to the Central Plains and the Korean Peninsula. With the contact between Turks and Persian Empire and Eastern Roman Empire and the ethnic migration in hundreds of years, stirrups gradually spread into Western Asia and Europe. It ultimately promoted the rise of the knighthood in medieval Europe.

有 / 无马镫骑乘体验装置：观众可以依次骑上有马镫和无马镫的马模型，比较有马镫和无马镫骑乘的稳定性差异
Riding Experience Device with or without Stirrups: The audience can ride on the horse model with or without stirrups in turns, and compare the stability difference between riding with and without stirrups

4. 马挽具
Horse Harness

马挽具是套在马匹上用于拉车的器具。大约在公元前2000年，两河流域出现了马车。中国出土的最早的马车是商代马车。古罗马贵族曾痴迷于疯狂的马车比赛。进入中世纪后，马成为普通百姓运货、拉车的好帮手。

The horse harness allows a horse to be driven. In around 2000 BC, a horse cart appeared in Mesopotamia. The earliest horse cart unearthed in China was in the Shang Dynasty. The nobility in ancient Rome was obsessed with horse racing. In the Middle Ages, horses gradually became a good helper for people to transport goods and pull cart.

颈带式挽具 / Neckband Harness

用颈带将马的颈部固定在衡上，通过衡和辕拖动车前进在古罗马和中国秦汉时期发展已比较成熟，其缺点是颈带压迫马的气管，影响马的呼吸。
The neck of the horse is fixed on the scale with the neck strap, and the horse is driven forward by the Heng and the shaft. The development of the neckband harnesses in ancient Rome and Qin and Han Dynasties has been relatively mature. The disadvantage is that the neckband compresses the horse's trachea and affects the horse's breathing.

胸带式挽具 / Chest Belt Harness

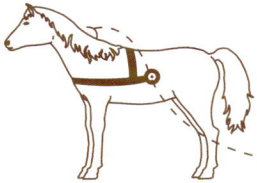

这种挽具是在马的胸部套一根带子，负重则由胸骨与锁骨承担，可以防止马呼吸不畅，缺点是难以发力，仅适合展示或牵引轻便负荷。古罗马和中国秦汉时期开始出现，现在仍在使用。
This kind of harness is a belt on the horse's chest, and the load is borne by the sternum and clavicle, which can prevent the horse from breathing obstructed. The disadvantage is that it is difficult to exert force, and is only suitable for displaying or pulling light loads. In ancient Rome, Qin and Han Dynasties this kind of harness began to appear and are still in use.

颈圈式挽具 / Collar Harness

早期颈带演化成用稻草、棕毛填充的套包，套包起到缓冲的作用，使马匹工作时更舒适。颈圈式挽具在中国汉代和古罗马时期已经出现。它在中国与胸带式挽具长期共存，在欧洲则是昙花一现，直到11世纪后才再次流行。
In the early stage, the neck band evolved into a kind of sheath filled with straw and brown hair, which played a buffer role and made the horses more comfortable when working. The collar harness was invented in the Han Dynasty and the ancient Rome period. It coexisted with chest belt harness for a long time in China, but it was a flash in the pan in Europe. It was not popular until the 11th century.

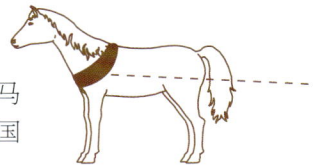

5. 丝路上的补给站 —— 驿站与商栈
Supply Stations on the Silk Road—Post Stations and Commercial Posts

在漫长而艰险的丝绸之路上，驿站和商栈是不可或缺的休憩、补给设施，为旅行者和商队提供食宿、更换牲畜甚至精神抚慰等服务。

驿站是古代供传递官府文书和军事情报的人或来往官员途中食宿、换马的场所。位于丝路上的驿站很多，现存比较有名的是汉代悬泉置遗址和明代鸡鸣驿。

丝路上，为长途跋涉的过路商队提供食宿的场所称为商栈。由于商队投宿期间的财产保护责任由商栈承担，因此商栈大都院墙高筑、大门加固，并建望楼以供瞭望值守，具有很强的防御性。历史上著名的商栈有伊朗迪尔加钦商栈、亚美尼亚奥贝里安商栈、乌兹别克斯坦阿巴迪马利克商栈等。

On the long and dangerous Silk Road, post stations and commercial posts are indispensable facilities for rest and supply. They provide accommodations, livestock replacement and even spiritual comfort services for the travellers and caravans.

In ancient China, the post station was a place for passing official documents and military intelligence personnel or officials on the way to board and lodging, and to change horses. There are many post stations on the Silk Road, among which the Xuanquanzhi site in the Han Dynasty and Jiming Post in the Ming Dynasty are more famous.

On the Silk Road, the place to provide food and accommodation for the long-distance caravan is called the commercial posts, and the property protection responsibility of the caravan during the lodging period is also borne by the commercial posts. Therefore, most of commercial posts have high walls, reinforced gates and watchtowers for lookouts, which are highly defensive. The famous commercial posts in history include Iran's Dilgachin Post, Armenian Oberian's Post, Uzbekistan's Abadi Malik Post.

建于1332年的亚美尼亚奥贝里安商栈
Armenian Oberian Commercial Post, Built in 1332

建于11世纪下半叶的乌兹别克斯坦阿巴迪马利克商栈
Uzbekistan Abadi Malik Commercial Post, Built in the Second Half of the 11th Century

汉代悬泉置遗址微缩复原模型：悬泉置遗址为中国汉代驿置机构，距今已有2000多年历史。遗址建筑包括房屋、马厩、院墙、烽燧、望楼等

Miniature Restoration Model of Xuanquanzhi Site in the Han Dynasty:The Xuanquanzhi site is a post office in the Han Dynasty, which has a history of more than 2000 years. There are many buildings, such as houses, stables, courtyard walls, beacon towers, watchtowers, etc.

建于公元3—7世纪的伊朗迪尔加钦商栈微缩模型
Miniature Restoration Model of Dilgachin Commercial Post, Iran, Built in the 3rd-7th Century A.D

鸡鸣驿：中国现存的唯一古驿站，始建于明朝初期，设有驿丞署、驿仓、把总署、公馆院、马号、戏楼及寺庙，堪称中国古代邮驿功能最全的驿站

Jiming Post : The only existing ancient post station in China. It was built in the early Ming Dynasty. It has a post office, a post warehouse, a general administration office, a residence, a stable, a theater and a temple. It can be regard as the most complete post station in ancient China

6. 中外驿道修筑方法对比

Comparison of Construction Methods of Post Roads between China and Foreign Countries

　　驿道修筑自古以来便是国家基础设施建设的重要方面。元代，平原地区的驿道通常是以沙土、砾石、炉渣等作为最下方的垫层，以夯土、石灰土或泥拌碎石作为路基层，最上层铺砌石板、碎石、卵石或砖石。山地驿道多在岩层上凿出路基，铺砌青石等作为路面。同时，除在转弯处加宽外，山地驿道还有石槛、石穴、护墙、栏杆等设施，以起防滑、缓冲等作用。

　　在古罗马，在被平整、夯实的生土层上铺砌约1米厚的土堤，土堤上铺一层沙土，沙土之上铺碎石，碎石上铺用较小的石块与石灰、火山灰组成的混凝土石子层，石子层上再铺用更小的碎石块与精细混凝土混合而成的垫层，最后铺砌平整的石板作为路面。为了便于雨天排水，路面中间微微凸起，道路两旁挖凿水沟，以利迅速排水。

Post road construction has been an essential aspect of national infrastructure construction since ancient times. In the Yuan Dynasty, the post road in plain areas was usually made of sand, gravel and slag as the bottom cushion, rammed earth, lime soil or mud mixed gravel as the road base, and the top surface course was paved with stone slab, gravel, pebble or masonry. Most of the mountain post roads are built on the rock bed and paved with bluestones. At the same time, in addition to widening at the turn, the mountain post road also has stone sill, cave, parapet, railing and other facilities to play a role of anti-skid and buffer.

In ancient Rome, a layer of 1-meter-thick embankment was paved on the levelled and compacted soil layer. A layer of sand was paved on the earth embankment, and gravel was paved on the sandy soil. The concrete gravel layer composed of small stones, lime and volcanic ash was paved on the gravel layer. The base layer formed of smaller crushed rocks and fine concrete was paved on the gravel layer. Finally, the flat stone slab was paved as the road surface. To facilitate the drainage of rainwater, the middle of the road is slightly raised, and ditches are dug on both sides of the road to facilitate rapid drainage.

元代驿道剖面结构微缩模型
The Model of Section Structure of Post Road in the Yuan Dynasty

古罗马大道剖面结构微缩模型
The Model of the Section Structure of the Avenue of Ancient Rome

7. 元代邮驿制度
Postal System in the Yuan Dynasty

　　中国的邮驿制度源远流长，在元代发展到鼎盛。元政府以大都（今北京）为中心，建立起以驿站为主体的马递网路和以急递铺为主体的步递网路，形成称雄一时的邮驿体系。四通八达的驿站网络构成了元政府的"神经和血液网络"，对维系国家对各地区的有效治理，尤其对发展边疆地区的交通起到了重要作用。

　　驿站在元代称为"站赤"。元朝驿站总数达1496座，分陆站和水站。陆站之间依靠人力和畜力运输。水站以舟楫运送来往使臣。元代共设水站424处，驿船近6000只。

China's postal system has a long history and reached its peak in the Yuan Dynasty. With Dadu (today's Beijing) as the center, the Yuan government established a horse delivery network with post stations and a running delivery network with express delivery posts, forming a post system that dominated for a long time. The post station network in all directions constitutes the "nerve and blood network" of the Yuan government, which plays an important role in maintaining the effective governance of the state over various regions, especially for the development of traffic in border areas.

The post station was called "Zhan Chi" in the Yuan Dynasty. There were 1496 post stations in the Yuan Dynasty, including land stations and water stations. Land stations rely on human and animal transport. The water station was transported by boat. In the Yuan Dynasty, there were 424 water stations and nearly 6000 post boats.

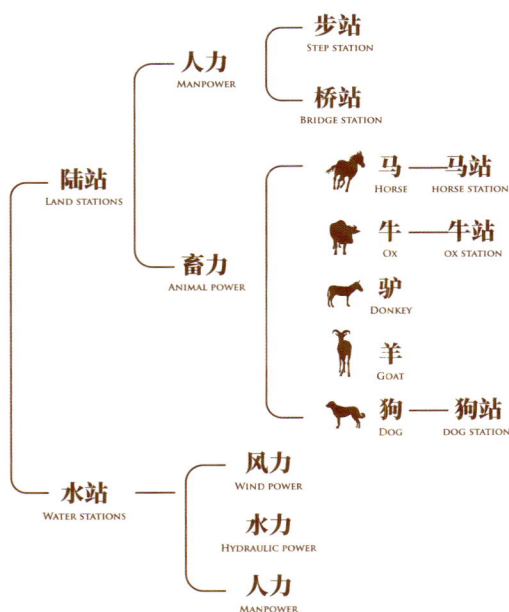

元代邮驿交通形式
Mail Stations and Transportation Forms of the Yuan Dynasty

8. 元代的特快专递 —— 急递铺
Speedpost in the Yuan Dynasty — Express Delivery Post

　　除了普通驿站，元代还设有专供军政大事的公文传递的急递铺。急递铺每5000米设一铺，传递速度约为普通邮驿的4倍，为200千米/天，加急时可达到400千米/天。据马可·波罗记载，早晨在大都采摘的新鲜水果，第二天晚上便可运到上都（位于今内蒙古），而这之间750千米的距离通常需要10多天才能完成运送。

　　急递铺起源于宋代的"急脚递"，由人工奔跑接力传递文书。所传文书用夹板保存以免褶皱，夹板外用油布覆盖以防御风雨。驿卒系上挂着铃铛的腰带，一路上以铃声警示路人退避，以确保通行速度。同时，远远传来的铃声会提示下一位驿卒做好准备，只要人一到站，等待的驿卒接过文件即刻出发，奔往下一站。这样日夜奔袭，可谓神速。

In addition to ordinary post stations, the Yuan Dynasty also had a unique delivery post for military and political affairs. An express delivery post is set up every 5 km, and the transmission speed is about four times of that of ordinary posts, which is 200 km / day, and it can reach 400 km / day in case of emergency. According to Marco Polo, fresh fruits picked in most of the mornings can be transported to Shangdu (now Inner Mongolia) the next night, and the distance of 750 km usually takes more than ten days to complete the transportation.

Express delivery posts originated from "jijiaodi" in the Song Dynasty, which was passed by a manual running relay. The documents were preserved with plywood to avoid wrinkles. The plywood was covered with oilcloth to protect against wind and rain. The postman wore a belt with a bell on his belt. Along the way, he warned passers-by to retreat and avoid collision, to ensure the passing speed. At the same time, the bell from afar will prompt the next courier to be ready. As soon as the person arrives, the waiting postman will take over the document and start to run to the next station.

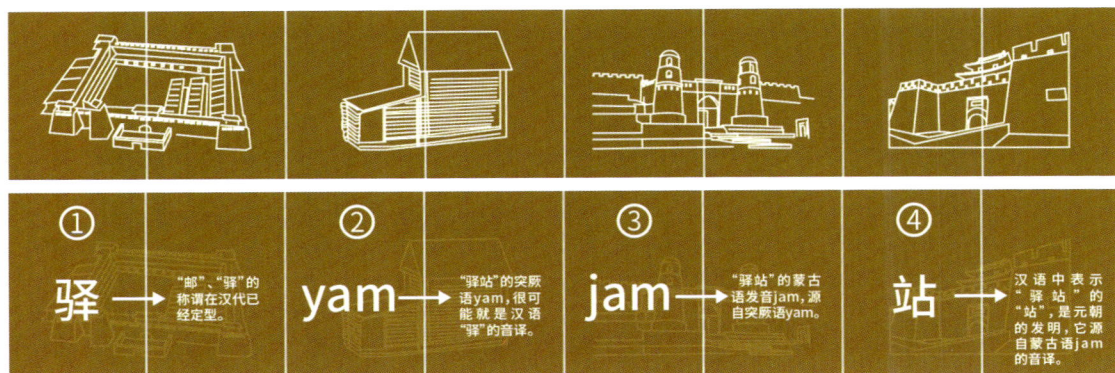

① 驿 → "邮"、"驿"的称谓在汉代已经定型。

② yam → "驿站"的突厥语yam，很可能就是汉语"驿"的音译。

③ jam → "驿站"的蒙古语发音jam，源自突厥语yam。

④ 站 → 汉语中表示"驿站"的"站"，是元朝的发明，它源自蒙古语jam的音译。

承载文化交流的"驿"与"站"：观众可通过互动方式了解汉语"驿""站"二字与突厥语、蒙古语的关系，感受驿路承载的多民族文化交流与融合

"Yi" and "Zhan" Carrying Language and Culture Communication:The visitors can understand the relationship between the Chinese characters "Yi" "Zhan" and the Languages Turkic and Mongolian through interaction, and feel the multi-ethnic cultural exchange and integration carried by the post road

9. 坎儿井
Karez

　　坎儿井是一种通过挖掘地下渠道，利用地下水实现自流灌溉的水利工程，它由竖井、地下暗渠、地面明渠和涝坝4部分组成。

　　坎儿井的优点在于对地下含水层的破坏性很小，流出的井水甘洌清澈，并且不会因炎热、大风而使水分大量蒸发，一年四季的水量比较稳定，能够有效避免地面盐碱化。

　　坎儿井起源于伊朗高原，11世纪由波斯经中亚传到现在新疆的吐鲁番和喀什等地，它将极度干旱的吐鲁番盆地变成了水草丰美、瓜果飘香的沙漠绿洲，孕育了丝绸之路上独特的绿洲文明。

Karez is an underground water diversion project built by people in arid areas in ancient times to obtain water for farming and living. It consists of four parts: vertical shaft, underground channel, surface open channel and waterlogging dam (reservoir).

It has many advantages: little damage to the underground aquifer, can avoid soil salinization, clear flowing well water, relatively stable amount of water throughout the year and so on.

Karez originated from the Iranian Plateau. In the 11th century, it spread from Persia through Central Asia to Turpan, Kashgar and other places in Xinjiang. It transformed the extremely arid Turpan Basin into a desert oasis with abundant water and grass, fragrant fruits and melons, and bred a unique oasis civilization along the Silk Road.

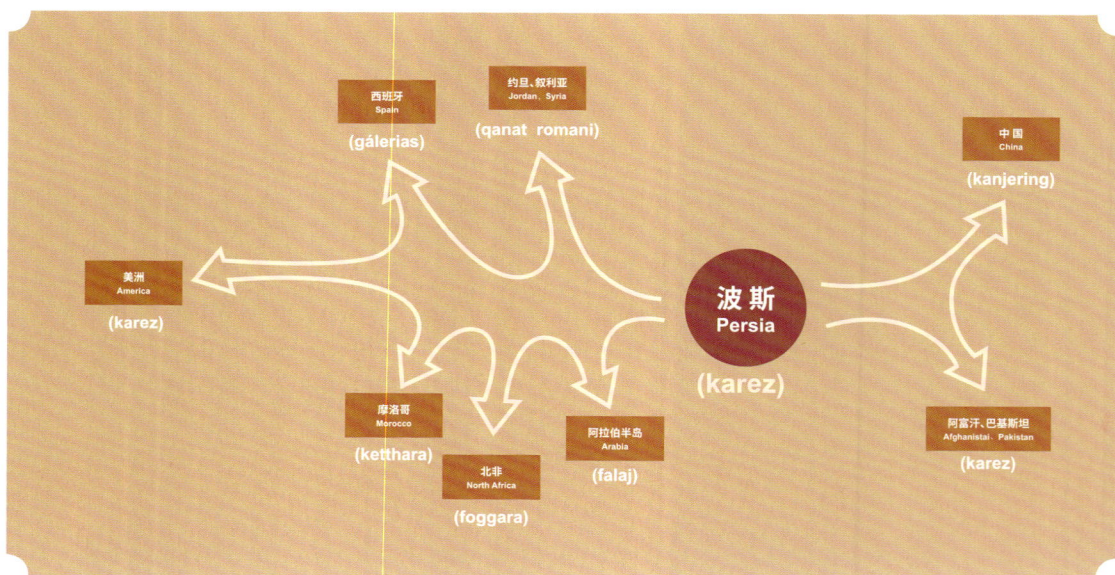

坎儿井传播路线图
The Spread of Karez

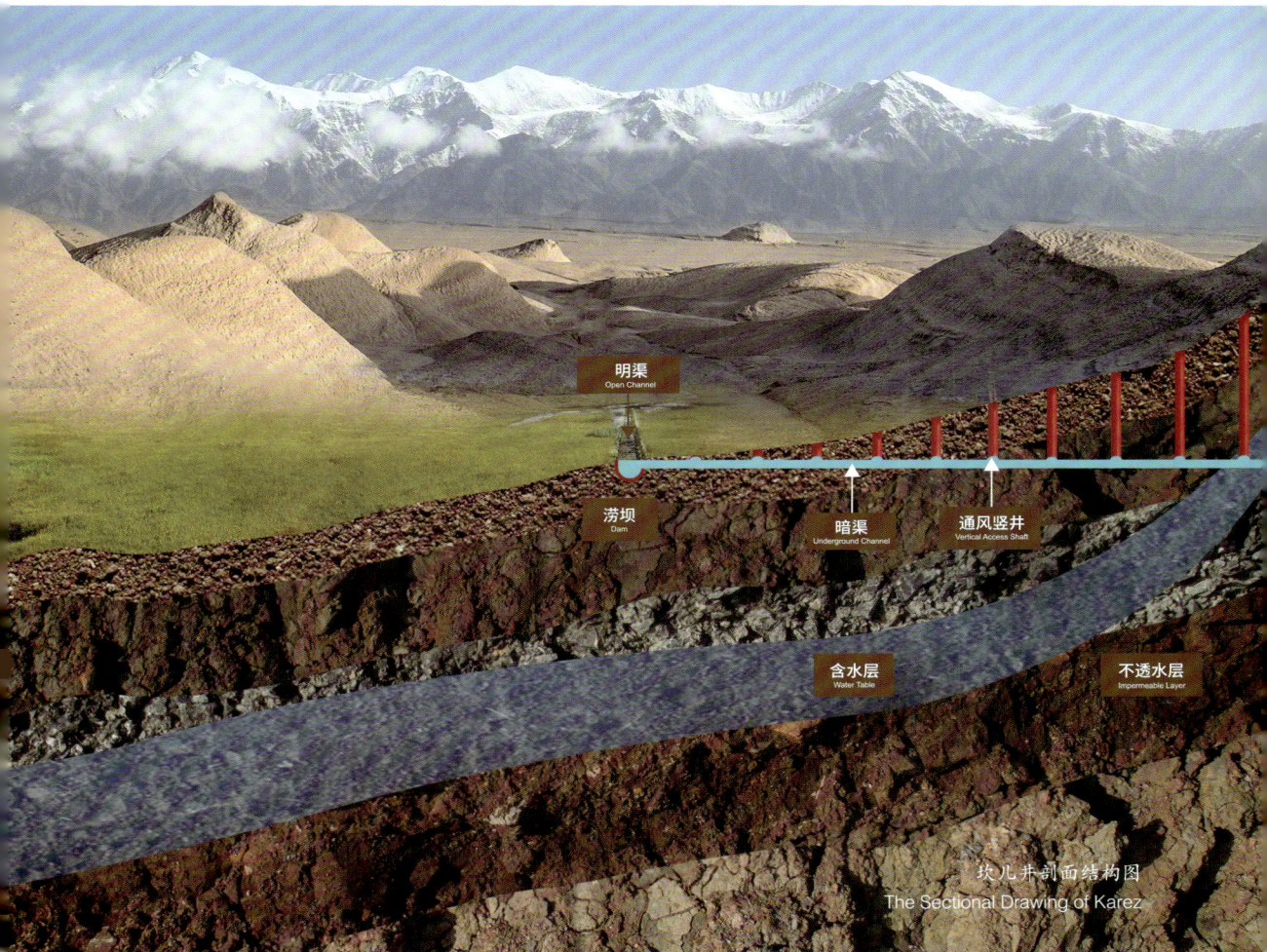

明渠
Open Channel

涝坝
Dam

暗渠
Underground Channel

通风竖井
Vertical Access Shaft

含水层
Water Table

不透水层
Impermeable Layer

坎儿井剖面结构图
The Sectional Drawing of Karez

新疆坎儿井
Xinjiang Karez

伊朗 Niavaran 坎儿井的出口处
Exit of Niavaran Karez in Iran

伊朗摩兹·德·阿巴德
坎儿井的地下暗渠
Underground Ditch in Moz
de Abad Karez in Iran

10. 中外古桥对比

Comparison of Ancient Bridges in China and Foreign Countries

　　桥梁是人们跨越山谷河流的特殊建筑。古人很早就开始利用不同材料建造各种类型的桥梁。

　　以石拱桥为例，拱将桥面荷载传递到河的两岸。多拱并列的连续拱使压力在各拱之间传递，从而跨越更长的距离。中国隋代建造的赵州桥和古罗马时期建造的法勃利克桥均为石拱桥，在桥型上都体现了古代拱桥从半圆拱到扁拱的变化，实现了低桥面和大跨度的双重目的。二者的区别在于赵州桥的两座小拱设在大拱拱肩上，法勃利克桥的小拱设在两拱之间的桥墩上，两种方法都起到了减轻桥身自重、减轻洪水压力的作用。

　　建于金代（1192年）的卢沟桥全长266.5米，11个孔拱券由两岸向桥心逐渐增大，中心孔跨径13.42米。初建于1177年、于1234年重建的法国圣贝内泽桥全长900米，为22孔石桥，后被洪水冲垮，至今余4孔。圣贝内泽桥拱的最大跨径为35.8米，桥墩上开小拱泄洪。两座桥均为连续多跨石拱桥，但净跨差距较大。

Bridges are a special building for people to cross the valley and river. Ancient people began to use different materials to build various types of bridges.

In the stone arch bridge, the arch transfers the bridge deck load to both sides of the river. For the continuous arch with multiple parallel arches, the force will be shared between the arches, to span a longer distance. Zhaozhou Bridge in China and Fabric Bridge in ancient Rome are both stone arch bridges, which reflect the change of ancient arch bridges from semicircular arches to flat arches in bridge types, realizing the dual purposes of the low bridge deck and large span. The difference between the two is that the two small arches of Zhaozhou Bridge are located on the large arch shoulder, and the small arch of Fabric Bridge is set on the pier between the two arches. Both methods have played a role in reducing the weight of the bridge body and reducing the flood pressure.

The Lugou Bridge, built in the Jin Dynasty (1192), has a total length of 266.5 meters. The 11 arch coupons gradually increase from both banks to the centre of the bridge. The centre hole has a span of 13.42 meters. The Saint-Bénézet Bridge in France was first built in 1177 and rebuilt in 1234. It is 900 meters long and is a 22-hole stone bridge. It was destroyed by floods, and only four holes remain. The maximum span of the arch of the Saint-Benezer Bridge is 35.8 meters, and a small arch is opened on the pier to discharge the flood. Both bridges are continuous multi-span stone arch bridges, but the net span gap is enormous.

赵州桥微缩模型
The Model of Zhaozhou Bridge

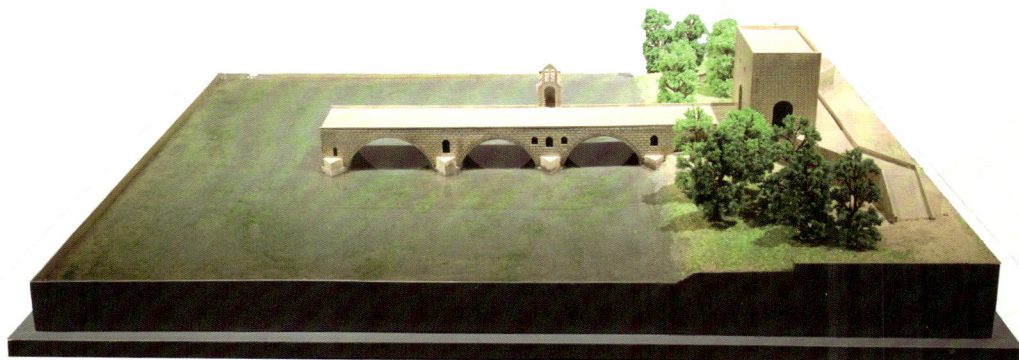

圣贝内泽桥微缩模型
The Model of the Saint-Bénézet Bridge

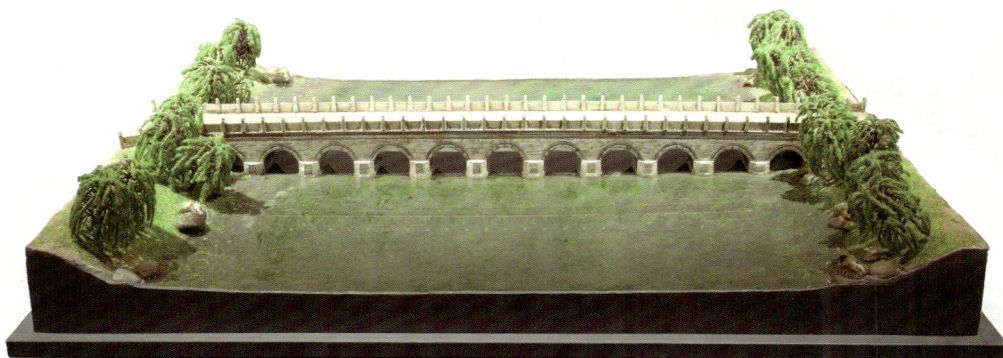

卢沟桥微缩模型
The Model of Lugou Bridge

11. 丝路沿途美食
Delicacies along the Silk Road

丝绸之路不仅加强了东西方的经贸交流，也促进了不同地区、不同民族间的饮食文化交流。

中华美食举世闻名，很多美食的食材源自国外。历史上沿着丝绸之路传入中国的农作物有豌豆、大蒜、香菜、苜蓿、菠菜、胡萝卜、花生、玉米、马铃薯、番薯、辣椒、西红柿等，它们极大地丰富了中国人的餐桌，对于解决中国粮食问题起到了重要作用。

随着中国东南沿海居民向南洋迁徙，豆腐、粿（米糕）、油条、粽子等中式美食被带到东南亚，对当地的饮食产生了影响。饺子、包子、面条等中国人的美食还被传到中亚及俄罗斯、意大利等欧洲地区，丰富了其他民族的饮食种类。

The Silk Road not only strengthened the economic and trade exchanges between the East and the West, but also promoted the catering cultural exchanges among different regions and nationalities.

Chinese cuisine is famous all over the world, and many of its ingredients come from abroad. Historically, the crops introduced into China along the Silk Road include pea, garlic, coriander, alfalfa, spinach, carrot, peanut, corn, potato, sweet potato, pepper, tomato, etc. They have greatly enriched the Chinese dining table and played an important role in solving China's food problem.

With the migration of southeast coastal residents to Southeast Asia, tofu, ke (rice cake), fried dough sticks, zongzi and other Chinese food were brought to Southeast Asia, which had an impact on local cuisine. Chinese delicacies such as dumplings, steamed buns and noodles were also spread to East Asia, Central Asia, Russia, Italy and other places, enriching the diet of other ethnic groups.

俄罗斯饺子
Pelmeni

俄罗斯饺子源于乌拉尔地区，意为"耳朵状的面包"，金帐汗国时期传入东欧地区。

Pelmeni originated from the Urals, meaning "ear-shaped bread," and were introduced to eastern European countries during the Golden Horde.

意大利饺子
Ravioli

意大利饺子出现于13世纪，起源未知。

Ravioli originated in the 13th century, with the origin being unknown.

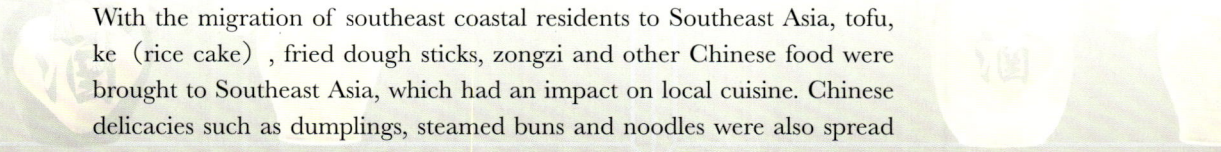

蒙古包子
Buuz

蒙古包子的发音来自汉语
"包子"。
Buuz originated from Chinese
"bun" (bao zi).

乌兹别克饺子
Manti

乌兹别克饺子的发音源于汉
语"馒头"。
Manti originated from Chinese
"steamed bun".

韩国饺子
Mandu

韩国饺子的发音来自汉语"馒
头",即中国南方对饺子或包子
的称呼。
Mandu originated from the Chinese
word "steamed bun" (man tou),
which means dumplings or buns in
South China.

中国饺子、包子
Chinese dumplings and
steamed stuffed buns

尼泊尔饺子
Momos

尼泊尔饺子的发音来自汉语"馍馍",通过
西藏传入南亚。
Momos originated from the Chinese "steamed
bread" (mo mo), which was introduced into
South Asia through Tibet.

中国饺子和包子的传播
The Spread of Chinese Dumplings and Steamed Stuffed Buns

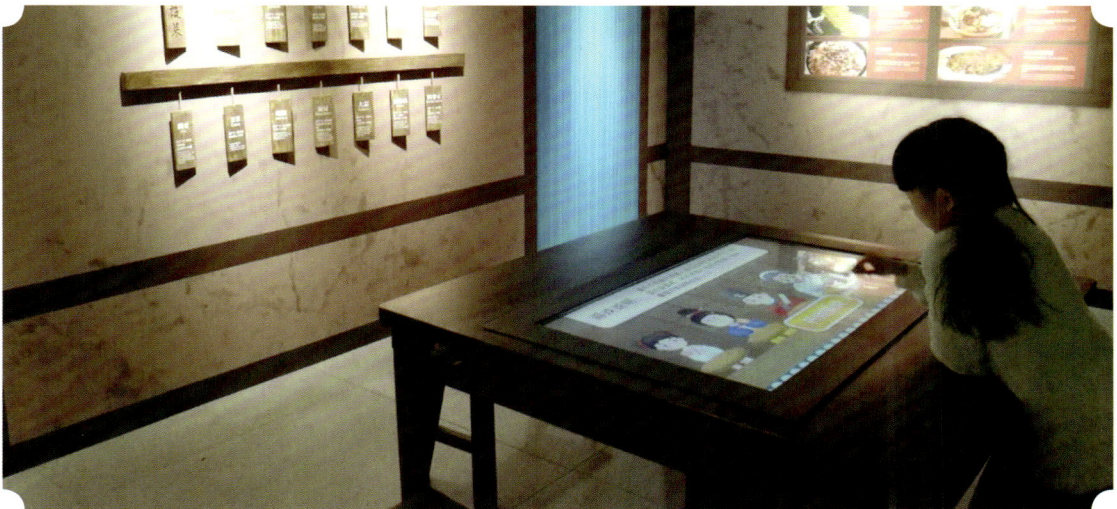

"丝路沿途美食"多媒体游戏:观众可在丝路驿站中"化身"店小二,给来自汉、唐、宋、元、明等历史时期的客人点餐,从
而了解不同时代传入中国的蔬菜
Multimedia Game of Delicacies along the Silk Road:In the Silk Road Post station, the audience can "incarnate" as a bartender to
prepare meals for guests from the Han, Tang, Song, Yuan, Ming and other historical periods, so as to understand the vegetables
introduced into China in different times

12. 坐具的变迁——胡床与交椅

Evolution of Sitting Device— Hu Bed and Folding Chair

　　早期人类的起居生活方式各有不同，欧洲人习惯于垂足而坐，而亚洲人则采用席地而坐的方式。大约在汉代，北方游牧民族将胡床从西域带到中原地带，使中国人的起居文化发生了从席地而坐到垂足而坐的变迁。

　　胡床：最早可能由古埃及人发明，是一种形似马扎而可以折叠的坐具，有两木相交，中间穿绳。

　　交椅：胡床在隋朝时改名为"交床"，在五代时逐渐发展成为交椅，宋代开始大量使用。交椅下部形似胡床，腿部呈交叉状，但增添了更舒适的弧形靠背和扶手。在等级森严的封建社会里，交椅只有皇室成员、达官显贵能坐，逐渐成为身份地位的象征。

Early human lifestyle was different. Europeans have been used to resting on a chair with feet down. In contrast, almost all the people in Asia have sat on the ground. In the Han Dynasty, the Hu bed of the northern nomads entered the Central Plains, and the seats began to undergo significant changes, sitting on chairs with feet down became popular.

Hu bed: it may have been invented in ancient Egypt. It is a kind of folding seat which looks like a campstool. There are two pieces of wood with a rope intersecting in the middle.

Folding chair: Hu bed was renamed Jiao bed in the Sui Dynasty, and gradually developed into a folding chair in the Five Dynasties. It was widely used in the Song Dynasty. The lower part of the folding chair looks like a Hu bed, and the legs are crossed, but a curved back and an armrest are added, making it more comfortable. In the feudal society with strict hierarchy, only royal family members, high-ranking officials and dignitaries could sit on a folding chairs, which gradually became the symbol of status.

胡床
Hu Bed

交椅
Folding Chair

13. 茶马古道
Ancient Tea Horse Road

  茶马古道被称作"南方丝绸之路"或"西南丝绸之路"，担负着中国西南地区内部及其与中国内地之间的贸易往来，也是连接中国与南亚次大陆的重要通道。茶马古道有3条主干线——川藏道、滇藏道、滇印道。

  茶马古道源于唐、宋时期边境实行的"茶马互市"，即中原以茶叶为商品，换取吐蕃、回纥、党项等游牧民族的马匹。茶马古道的运输方式有牦牛驮运、人力背运、马匹驮运等多种形式。犹如丝绸并非丝绸之路的唯一商品，茶、马也无法囊括茶马古道上丰富的商品交易。通过茶马古道，川、滇和中原出产的茶叶、丝绸、布料、铁器以及其他生产生活资料源源不断地运往西藏和南亚，而西藏和南亚盛产的黄金、皮革及虫草、贝母等珍贵药材也由此销往中原。

The Ancient Tea Horse Road is called the Southern Silk Road or the Southwest Silk Road. It not only undertakes the trade between southwestern China and the Central Plains of China but also serves as an important corridor connecting China and the South Asian subcontinent. There are main roads of the three Ancient Tea Horse Roads in southwestern China—Sichuan-Tibet Road, Yunnan-Tibet Road and Yunnan-India Road.

The name The Ancient Tea Horse Road originated from the "Tea horse trade" in the Tang and Song dynasties, which means the Chinese bartered tea for horses with nomadic groups like Tubo, Huihe and Dangxiang. There were various ways of transportation including porter, yak and horse on the Ancient Tea Horse Roads. Just like the silk, which was not the only commodity of the "silk road", tea and horses were also a part of the abundant commodities being traded in this region. The Tibetan region's primary demand for products from the Central Plains were tea, silk, cloth, iron and other living materials. At the same time, the gold, leather and Chinese caterpillar fungus from Tibet enjoyed great popularity in the Central Plains.

茶马古道展项
Exhibit of the Ancient Tea Horse Road

14. 丝绸之路上的乐器
Musical Instruments on the Silk Road

    汉代，随着丝绸之路的开通，西域音乐伴随乐曲、乐器、音乐家等传入中原，与中国本土音乐相互交融。琵琶、箜篌、筚篥、胡琴、腰鼓、铙钹等乐器自西向东陆续传入。其中，琵琶作为领奏乐器在唐代大放异彩，至今已成为"中国民族乐器之王"。

    中国并不是丝绸之路音乐交流的终点，华乐东传的故事同样精彩。不同音乐在这里交融后，继续向东传播。琵琶经中国文化的浸润，遍及汉字文化圈，发展出日本琵琶、朝鲜琵琶和越南琵琶。另外，中国本土的阮咸、平纹琴等乐器的东传也影响了朝鲜半岛及日本的音乐文化。

In the Han Dynasty, with the opening of the Silk Road, music, musical instruments, musicians from the western regions was introduced into China. Pipa, konghou, Bili Pipe, huqin, waist drum, cymbals and other musical instruments were introduced from West to East. Among them, pipa, as a leading musical instrument, flourished in the Tang Dynasty, and has become "the king of Chinese national musical instruments".

China is not the end of the Silk Road music exchange. The story of Chinese music spreading eastward is also fantastic. After different music blends here, it continues to spread eastward. Through the infiltration of Chinese culture, Pipa has spread throughout the cultural circle of Chinese characters and developed into Japanese pipa, Korean Pipa and Vietnamese pipa. In addition, the spread of ruan xian, ping wen and other musical instruments in China also influenced the music culture of the Korean Peninsula and Japan.

榆林25窟南壁《观无量寿经变》中的丝路乐器
In Paintings of the Amitāyurdhyāna Sutra in Cave 25 of Yulin Brotto, the Music Performer Hold Silk Road Instruments

15. 琵琶的前世今生
The Past and Present Life of Pipa

　　汉代，西域乐器传入中原，其中琵琶的影响最深远。中国最早被称为"琵琶"的乐器出现在秦朝，被称为"秦琵琶"。魏晋时期，"竹林七贤"中的阮咸擅长弹奏秦琵琶，人们便用他的名字来命名这种乐器，称之为"阮咸"，简称"阮"，"琵琶"这个称呼则让给了传入乐器——胡琵琶。胡琵琶有两种形制，分别为五弦琵琶和曲项琵琶。受中原文化影响，曲项琵琶的音箱逐渐变薄，曲项逐渐伸直，形成了现代琵琶的形制。同时，琵琶的弹奏方式由横抱、用拨片弹奏演变为竖抱、用手指弹奏，体现了中国人儒雅含蓄的文化气质。

In the Han Dynasty, Western musical instruments were introduced into China, and pipa had the most profound influence. China's earliest known "Pipa" appeared in the Qin Dynasty, known as "Qin pipa". During the Wei and Jin Dynasties, Ruan Xian, one of the "Seven Sages of the bamboo grove", was good at playing Qin pipa. People named this instrument after him, and called it "Ruan Xian" or "Ruan" for short. The name "Pipa" was given to the introduced musical instrument, Hu pipa. There are two forms of Hu Pipa: five-string Pipa and curved pipa. Influenced by the culture of China, the soundbox of curved pipa gradually thinned, and the curved part straightened out, forming the shape of the modern pipa. At the same time, the way of playing pipa has changed from horizontal holding and plucking to vertical holding and finger playing, which reflects the refined and implicit cultural temperament of Chinese people.

曲项琵琶（四弦、梨形音箱、琴头弯曲）
Curved Pipa (Four Strings, Pear Shaped Soundbox, Curved Head)

五弦琵琶（五弦、梨形音箱、琴头笔直）
Five String Pipa (Five String, Pear Shaped Soundbox, Straight Head)

阮咸（四弦、圆形音箱、琴头笔直）
Ruan Xian (Four String, Round Soundbox, Straight Head)

漫游古代中国

Wandering around Ancient China

沿着丝绸之路，风尘仆仆的丝路商旅来到中国腹地，无不惊叹于这里的繁荣与富庶。繁华的街市、奇巧的百工、高妙的技艺、精准的历算……令人目不暇接。 马可·波罗也在这里见到了具有陌生感的熟悉事物。人同此心，心同此理，面对相似的技术问题，东西方往往有相近的解决方案。那些与西方迥异的技术解决方案被有心人介绍到西方。于是，来自各文明的先进成果在这里融会贯通，东方的原创科技也通过丝绸之路走向世界。

　　在"漫游古代中国"展区，观众可以徜徉在"前店后厂"式的绸缎铺、陶瓷坊、南纸店，可以了解到丝绸、陶瓷、造纸术与印刷术的科技原理、工艺流程，还可以亲身体验纺织、古法造纸、拓印和木版水印等中国传统技艺。

Along the Silk Road, merchants came to the hinterland of China and were amazed by its prosperity. Bustling streets, masterly craftsmen, excellent skills and accurate calendar dazzled visitors. Marco Polo also saw familiar things with a strange appearance here. People feel and think alike on some matters. When faced with similar technical problems, the East and the West often have similar solutions. Technical solutions that are different from those in the West were introduced to the West. As a result, the advanced achievements of various civilizations were interwoven here, and the original technologies of the East were introduced to the world through the Silk Road.

In the exhibition area of "Wandering around Ancient China", visitors can wander in the silk store, ceramic store and paper store where there were factories in the back. They can learn about the technological principles and processes of silk, ceramics, paper making and printing, and experience traditional Chinese techniques such as textiles, ancient papermaking, rubbing and woodblock printing.

1. 东西方的锁
The Lock of the East and the West

东西方的锁各有其独立的发源。中国是东方锁具的发源地，其后传到朝鲜、日本、越南等地。西方锁具的发源地是两河流域及古埃及，以后传到古希腊、古罗马，再由欧洲传到美洲。

The locks of the East and the West have their own origins. China was the birthplace of the lock of the East, which later spread to Korea, Japan and Vietnam. The birthplace of Western locks is Mesopotamia and ancient Egypt. Later they spread to ancient Greece and Rome, and then from Europe to America.

古代中国簧片挂锁 / Reed Padlock in Ancient China

簧片锁是古代中国最典型的锁具。上锁时，锁栓上张开的簧片会撑开并抵住锁体内壁，以防止锁被打开；若要打开，必须插入钥匙，使钥匙头挤压簧片而打开锁栓。

The reed padlock is the most typical lock in ancient China. When locking, the open spring on the lock bolt will stretch out and bear against the inner wall of the lock to prevent the lock from being opened. You must insert the key so that the key head squeezes the spring leaf and move it into the lock bolt.

古代中国组合挂锁 / Combination Padlock in Ancient China

组合锁为横式圆柱体形状，在圆柱的轴芯上排列数只转轮，每只转轮的表面刻着同样数目的文字，只要所有转轮上的文字转到预定位置，使文字形成特定的字串，即可开锁。

The combination padlock is in the shape of a horizontal cylinder. Several runners are arranged on the axis core of the cylinder. The surface of each runner is engraved with the same number of characters. It can be unlocked as long as the Chinese characters on all runners form a specific string.

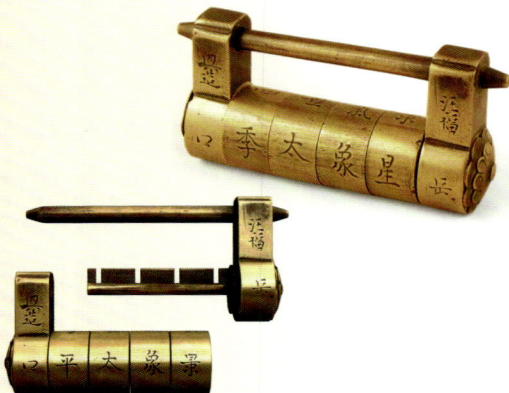

古埃及木栓锁 / Wooden Bolt Lock in Ancient Egypt

　　古埃及木栓锁的门固垂直固定在木门上，钥匙呈牙刷状，一端有数根配合锁栓位置和形状的小木栓。开锁时，把钥匙经由门闩中的槽道插入至定位后再往上滑动，把对应的锁栓顶离门闩，就可水平滑动门闩开锁。

The fixture of the wooden bolt lock in ancient Egypt was fixed vertically on the wooden door. The key was in the shape of a toothbrush, and several small wooden bolts were matching the position and shape of the deadbolt at one end. When unlocking, you should insert the key into the position through the slot in the latch, and then slide it upward. When the corresponding deadbolt is pushed away from the latch, the latch can be slid horizontally to open the lock.

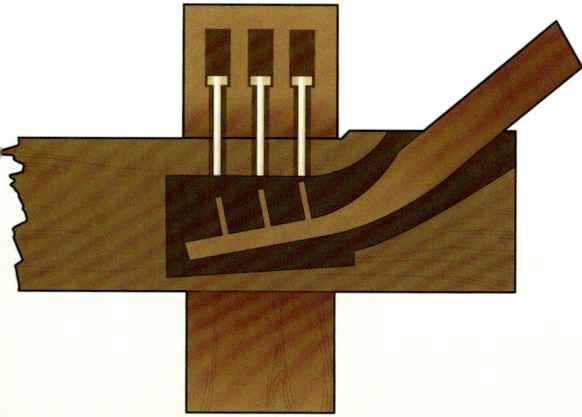

古罗马凸块锁 / Ancient Roman Warded Lock

　　凸块锁是古罗马时期制作的，在锁的内部有一个叫"凸块"的障碍，凸块一般很复杂，如果是正确的钥匙就可以通过钥匙上的空隙形状，不碰到凸块进行转动，进而就可以开锁。

The warded lock was made in ancient Rome. There is an obstacle called a convex block in the lock. The convex block is usually very complex. If it is the right key, you can turn the key without touching the convex block, and open the lock smoothly.

2. 丝绸工艺流程
Silk Process

　　中国是最早养蚕缫丝和发明丝织的国家。大约公元前3000年，中国人已经成功驯化了野生桑蚕，使其成为可以饲养的家蚕，并利用蚕丝织出美丽的丝绸织物。随着蚕桑业和丝织技术的发展，逐渐形成了从蚕桑到丝绸的完整体系。

　　丝绸的制作要经过采桑、养蚕、缫丝、络丝、染色、整经、摇纬、织造、剪帛等步骤。用采得的嫩桑叶喂育的蚕生长30～40天后会吐丝结茧，将蚕茧浸在热盆汤中，用手抽丝，生丝经过精炼和染色处理，选取所需的数量绕到丝筒上，再装在织机上即可以织造出精美的丝绸。

China is the first country to raise silkworms for reeling and to invent silk weaving. By about 3000 BC, the Chinese had successfully domesticated wild silkworms into homebred silkworms and made beautiful silk fabrics from silk. In the development of sericulture and silk weaving technology, a complete system including silkworm breeding, mulberry growing and silk weaving was gradually formed.

The production of silk must go through ten steps, such as collecting mulberry and raising silkworms, reeling silk, winding, dyeing, warping, wefting, weaving, and silk cutting, etc. Silkworms fed with young mulberry leaves will spin cocoons after 30—40 days of growth. Soak the cocoons in hot pot soup and draw the silk by hand. The raw silk is finished by refining and dyeing, and the desired quantity is selected and wound on the silk drum. When it is assembled on the loom, fine silk can begin to be woven.

丝织工艺流程图
Silk Process

中国古代织造技术的最高成就——
大花楼织机的微缩模型
The Highest Achievement in Ancient
Chinese Weaving Technology-A
Miniature Model of Large Double
Drawloom

3. 丝绸制品
Silk Products

丝绸根据织物组织、经纬线组合、加工工艺和绸面表现形状，可分绉、缎、绫、纱、罗、绒、锦、绢等共14类。比如，锦是二组或二组以上经线或纬线用重组织形成的质地较厚实、外观丰富多彩的提花丝织物。织锦技术始于西周。唐代以前主要采用经线显花，即经锦。唐代以后由于丝绸之路的发展，受西域纺织技术的影响，出现了以彩色纬线显花的纬锦。后进一步发展出以经线的经面效应组织作为织物的地纹，由不同色彩纬线显现花纹的经纬显花锦。

According to the fabric structure, combination of warp and weft, processing technology and silk surface, silk can be divided into crepe, satin, ghatpot, yarn, Luo, velvet, brocade, juan silk, etc. There are 14 categories in total.For instance, Brocade is two or more sets of warp or weft, formed by heavy structure and with thick texture, jacquard fabric with rich appearance. Brocade technology originated from the Western Zhou Dynasty. Before the Tang Dynasty, patterns were mainly displayed by warp silk yarns, which was called warp-patterned brocade. After the Tang Dynasty, with the development of the Silk Road and influence of the textile technology of the West, the weft-patterned brocade appeared. After further development, the warp surface was used as the ground grain of the fabric, and the warp and weft flower brocade of the pattern was expressed by different color weft lines.

锦：二组或二组以上经线或纬线用重组织形成的质地较厚实、外观丰富多彩的提花丝织物
Brocade : Two or more sets of warp or weft, formed by heavy structure and with thick texture, jacquard fabric with rich appearance

纱：全部或部分应用纱组织的织品，由甲、乙经丝每隔一纬丝扭绞而成
Yarn : A fabric made entirely or partly of yarn fabric. It is formed by twisting the A and B warp threads every other weft

缎：采用缎纹组织形成的丝织物

Satin : A silk fabric formed of satin weave

绫：一种以斜纹组织为基本组织的单层织物

Ghatpot : A kind of single-layered fabric with twill structure

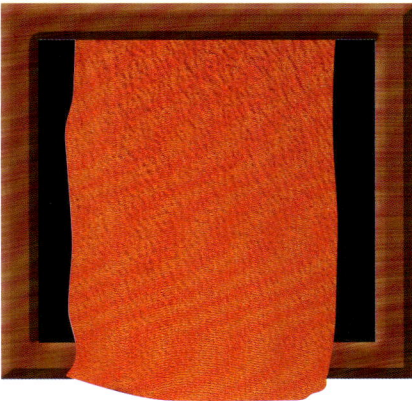

绉：采用加强捻丝线以平纹组织或绉组织为基本组织
的丝织物

Crepe : The silk fabric that uses reinforced silk yarns as the
basic structure of plain weave or crepe structure

绢：古代对质地紧密轻薄、细腻平挺的平纹类丝织物
的通称

Juan Silk : A general term for plain, silky fabrics that are
compact, light and smooth

罗是经线采用绞组组织，使经线明显扭转形成孔眼的
轻薄透孔丝织物

Luo : A thin silk fabric with pores. It applies twisted group
structure on warps to form a perforation

绒是织物有一组经线或纬线采用具有规律的起绒组织
交织于一般经纬线之中的，并在织物表面形成毛茸或
毛圈的纺织品

Velvet: There is a set of warp or weft threads which are
interwoven into the general warp and weft threads with
regular velvet organizations, and form a furry or terry on the
surface of the fabric

4. 丝绸技术的传播
The Outflow of the Silk Technology

中国是丝绸的故乡，丝绸织品因其工艺技术复杂，曾被中国垄断数百年。

汉代的"传丝公主"将蚕种密藏于所戴丝绵帽里，顺利将蚕种带到和亲的于阗国，于阗国便逐渐成为著名的丝织产地。在很长时间里，丝绸还承担着支付戍卒薪水、购买马匹等重要的货币功能。随着东西方贸易的发展，丝绸在西方各国盛行，古希腊和古罗马的王室、贵族均以拥有丝绸服饰而自豪。

几千年前，丝绸沿着丝绸之路从中国传向欧洲，丝绸因此也成了东方文明的传播者和丝绸之路的象征。

庞贝壁画之《花神》上身着丝绸的女子
A Woman in Silk in the Mural of Pompell
Flower God

China is the hometown of silk. For hundreds of years, Silk fabrics were monopolized by China because of their complicated technology.

Chuansi Princess of Han Dynasty hid the silkworm eggs in the silk cotton hat she was wearing, and successfully brought them to Khotep where she was going to get married with the young king there. Since then, Khotan gradually became a famous silk-producing area. For a long time, silk also served as an essential currency role, such as paying soldiers' salaries and buying horses. With the development of trades between the East and the West, silk became very popular in Western countries. The royal families and nobles of ancient Greece and Rome were all proud of their silk costumes.

Thousands of years ago, the silk travelled along the Silk Road from China to Europe. Therefore the silk became the communicator of Oriental civilization and the symbol of the Silk Road.

"传丝公主"画版
A Chuansi Princess Painting

5. 东方丝绸的异域风情
Exotic Style of Eastern Silk

　　随着丝绸之路的畅通，来自中亚、西亚的各种动物、植物、神、人物等异域纹样纷纷出现在丝绸面料上。中国人在模拟仿制和来样加工的过程中，把异域的美学思想、设计思维、表现方法、工艺技巧等潜移默化地融入中国传统丝绸图案设计中，丰富了中国传统丝绸图案的艺术表现力。比如，吐鲁番阿斯塔那古墓群出土的"方格兽纹锦"中的狮子，由原本刚烈威猛的西方猛兽变为更符合东方文化审美的温柔形象。

With the opening and communication of the Silk Road, exotic objects such as animals, plants, gods, and figures from Central Asia and West Asia appeared on silk fabrics and objects. In the process of simulating imitation and sample processing, the Chinese have subtly integrated exotic aesthetic thoughts, design thinking, expression methods and craftsmanship into the traditional Chinese silk pattern design, enriching the artistic expression of traditional Chinese silk patterns: For instance, the lion in the "Square Animal Pattern" unearthed from the ancient tomb of Astana in Turpan. The originally fierce and powerful Western beast became gentler and lovelier, and more in line with the aesthetics of Eastern culture.

方格兽纹锦：织物中的狮子卧伏、吐舌、弄眼，乖巧可爱
Square Animal Pattern : In the form of lying, tongue-in-cheek, and eye-catching, the lion is cute and gentle in Square Animal Pattern

四骑士狩猎纹锦：图案中的骑士为穿着唐服的胡人形象
Four Hunting Knights Pattern : The knights in the image are western knights wearing Tang costumes

花树对鹿纹锦：织物中的"十字唐草纹"曾在古希腊十分流行
Flower Tree with a Pair of Deer Pattern : The symmetrical cross-grass pattern around the circle is very popular in ancient Greece

胡王锦：图案中有胡人牵骆驼的形象，并带有"胡王"的字样
Huwangjin : There was the image of a western traveler holding a camel and the word "Huwang"

6. 丝路沿途服装

Clothes along the Silk Road

　　丝绸之路沿线各国，如希腊、土耳其、波兰等，都有自己传统的民族服装，服装在注重实用性的基础上还体现了各国的不同文化。

　　个性浪漫、奔放的古希腊人使服装具备了优雅、飘逸、高贵等特点。比如，我们看到的奥运会圣火采集仪式上古希腊女祭司穿的束腰长袍就是古希腊的一种传统服装。采用纱质、缎质面料及雪纺等面料，穿在身上有厚坠感，整体设计旨在凸显上身，一根长长的带子系在腰间，胸线以下为直筒轮廓，素雅的白色为其代表色。

Countries along the Silk Road, such as Greece, Turkey and Poland, have their own traditional national costumes. Apart from its focus on practicality, clothing also reflects the different cultures of various countries.

The romantic and unrestrained ancient Greeks bring elegance, grace and nobility into their clothing. For example, the costume worn by the ancient Greek priestess during the Olympic torch ceremony was a tunic robe, which was a traditional costume of ancient Greece. Using yarn, satin, chiffon and other fabrics, it felt thick when worn. With a long strap tied around the waist, the overall design is to highlight the upper body. Below the chest line is a straight silhouette, and the elegant white is its representative color.

智能穿衣镜：观众可通过该展项模拟试穿不同民族的服饰

Smart Dressing Mirror : Visitors can try on costumes of different nationalities through this exhibition item

7. 如何辨别丝绸
How to Distinguish Silk

仿真丝是将涤纶纤维长丝经过特殊处理而成，其具备类似真丝的性能。辨别真丝和人造真丝可通过对折、触摸、摩擦、拉扯、燃烧等方法。

1. 对折：真丝具备高弹性，对折后基本上不会留下折痕，可以恢复原状，光滑如初。人造真丝不具备这样的弹性，容易产生折痕。

2. 触摸：真丝手感柔软，穿着滑爽，一般的化纤织物却不具备这个特点。

3. 摩擦：用力摩擦织物，除真丝外，其他织物不会发出"绢鸣"声。

4. 拉扯：挑选出几条纱，用水浸湿，用力拉扯，断在湿处的为人造纤维，断处长短不一的为真丝。

5. 燃烧：真丝燃烧时无明火，犹如毛发的气味，灰烬呈微粒状，可捏碎。仿真丝一般会有火苗产生，发出塑料的气味，并且留下固体胶块物。

We can identify and distinguish real silk and imitated silk by folding, touching, rubbing, pulling, burning, etc.

1. By folding in half: Silk has high elasticity. Basically, no creases will be left on silk after being folded in half, and it can be restored to its original shape and smooth as before. In contrast, artificial silk does not have such elasticity and is prone to creases.

2. By touching: Silk is soft and smooth, yet chemical & blended fabric doesn't have this feature.

3. By rubbing: Rub the fabric strongly. If it's not silk, it won't create a "beep" sound.

4. By pulling: Pick a few yarns, soak them into the water, and pull hard. If they break at the soaked place, they're man-made fibers; if the broken parts have different lengths, they're made of silk.

5. By burning: When burning the silk, there is no open flame, but emitting the smell of hair. The ashes are in the form of particles and can be crushed. However artificial silk has flame while burning and will emit a plastic smell, leaving a solid rubber block.

对折

对折：真丝对折后基本不会留下折痕
Folding:While the silk is folded in half, it basically does not leave creases

触摸

触摸：触摸真丝，手感柔软
Touching:When touching silk, it feels soft

摩擦

摩擦：用力摩擦两层真丝，会发出"绢鸣"声
Rubbing:Rub two layers of the silk, it will make a "beep" sound

8. 传入中国的棉纺织技术
Cotton Textile Technology Introduced to China

唐代，棉花从印度传入中国的海南岛等地，中国的棉纺织技术也由此得以发展。

中国棉纺织业的先驱是13世纪杰出的棉纺技术革新家——黄道婆，她将自己在海南学到的纺纱技术进行改革，创造出一整套先进的棉纺工具和棉纺技术。她把原来弹棉花用的小竹弓和手指改为用大弓椎击法，原来纺纱用的单锭纺车改为三锭纺车，大大提高了纺线的效率，使棉花作为原料大量用于织布成为可能。在织染方面，她教会人们怎样用错纱、配色、综线、挈花等方法织出各种美丽的图案。她还教当地妇女怎样织作被面，使得"乌泥泾被"声名鹊起，享誉全国。

In the Tang Dynasty, cotton was introduced from India to Hainan Island and other places in China. China's cotton textile technology was thus developed.

Huangdaopo is the pioneer of the Chinese cotton textile industry and an outstanding cotton textile technology innovator in the 13th century. By reformation the cotton textile technology she learned in Hainan, she created a set of advanced cotton spinning tools and cotton spinning technology. Originally people used small bamboo bows and fingers to fluff cotton filler. She changed them into big bow vertebrae. She also changed the original single spinning machine into the three-spinning machine, which greatly improved the efficiency of the spinning line. Thus it was possible that cotton could be widely used as the raw material in weaving. In terms of weaving and dyeing, she taught people to make yarns, combine colors and healds, weave flowers and other beautiful patterns. She also taught local women how to weave quilts, making the Wuni Brook famous throughout the country.

Using advanced cotton textile technology, people use natural fibers to weave fabrics of various materials, such as silk, cotton, hemp, and wool, etc. These fabrics are generally comfortable to wear, breathable and warm. Fabrics such as polyester woven with man-made fibers have the characteristics of firmness, wrinkle resistance and abrasion resistance.

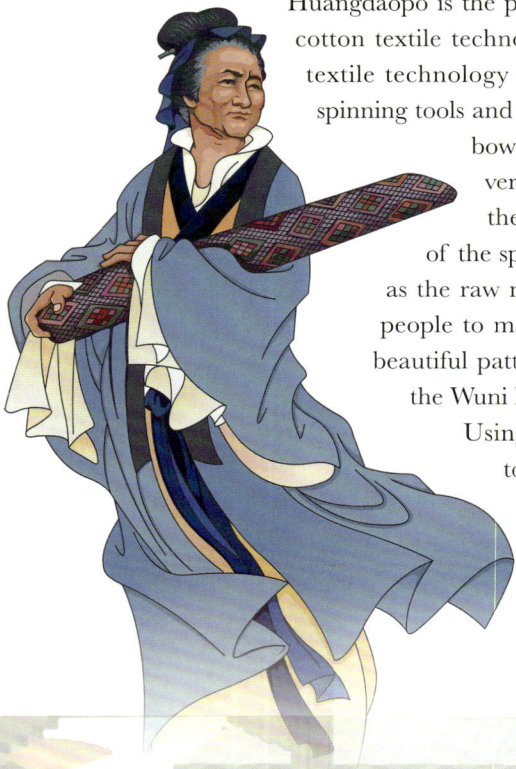

黄道婆：中国棉纺织业先驱
Huangdaopo:The pioneer of the Chinese cotton textile industry

手摇纺车
Hand-Operated Spinning Wheel

9. 造纸术
Papermaking

　　纸发明之前，人类采用过甲骨、泥版、缣帛等各种各样的书写记事材料，但都或昂贵，或笨重，直到西汉时期，中国人发明了造纸术，才有了轻便的书写载体——纸。

　　纸的主要原料取自植物纤维。中国人最早使用的造纸原料是大麻和苎麻。东汉时期，蔡伦开辟了一种新的造纸材料来源——树皮。魏晋南北朝时期又出现了以青藤皮为原料的藤纸。唐以后，以竹子为原料的竹纸兴起，并且发展极为迅速，很快取代麻纸、藤纸，从宋元到明清时期一直居于统治地位。除此之外，草也是造纸的原料之一。

Before the invention of paper, humans used a variety of writing materials, such as oracle bones, clay plates scorpions, etc. However, some of these materials were too expensive, others too bulky. It was not until the Western Han Dynasty when the Chinese invented papermaking that lighter and more convenient paper for writing was available.

The main raw material of paper is taken from plant fibers. The first papermaking materials used by the Chinese are hemp and ramie. During the Eastern Han Dynasty, Cai Lun developed a new raw material for papermaking-bark. During the Wei, Jin and Southern and Northern Dynasties, vine paper made of green vine skin appeared. After the Tang Dynasty, bamboo paper made of bamboo aroused and developed rapidly. It quickly replaced the ramie paper and vine paper and dominated the paper market from the Song and Yuan Dynasties to the Ming and Qing Dynasties. In addition, grass was also one of the raw materials for papermaking.

树皮
Bark

麻
Ramie Fiber

竹子
Bamboo

草
Grass

10. 造纸工艺流程
Papermaking Process

    《天工开物》一书中详细记载了明代造竹纸的工艺流程，即分为斩竹漂塘、煮楻足火、荡料入帘、覆帘压纸、透火焙干五大步骤。

    ①斩截嫩竹，放入池塘，浸泡百日以上，使之青皮去除。②将竹料拌入石灰水浸在楻桶中蒸煮，用塘水漂洗过后再次进行蒸煮，如此反复进行十几天，便可实现纸料的除胶步骤。③竹料纤维充分分解，经捣烂后用水调成纸纤维的悬浮液，便可进行抄纸。④竹帘在水槽中抄纸成功后要将竹帘翻过去，使纸张叠积放置至千张左右，再用木板重压挤去水分。⑤最后将湿纸逐张扬起，并焙干，即得成纸。

In *Tiangong Kaiwu*, there is a detailed record of bamboo paper manufacturing process in Ming Dynasty, that is: bamboo cutting and soaking, cooking a full fire, swinging into the curtain, covering paper and drying thoroughly.

① Cut the tender bamboo, put it into the pond, soak it for more than 100 days, and wash away the green skin of the bamboo. ② Mix the bamboo material with lime water later and immerse them in a simmering bucket for boiling. Then, the materials are rinsed in a pond and cooked again. And this is repeated for more than ten days, thus the paper materials can be degummed. ③ As a result, bamboo fiber is fully decomposed. After being mashed, the bamboo fiber is adjusted with water and become paper fiber suspension, and then papermaking can be carried out. ④ After the bamboo curtain has successfully made paper in the sink, the bamboo curtain should be reversed. Therefore the paper is stacked and placed about a thousand sheets. Then put a heavy board on top to press and squeeze most of the water. ⑤ Then the wet paper is lifted one by one. After drying, it becomes paper.

❶

斩竹漂塘
Bamboo Cutting and
Soaking

2

煮楻足火
Cooking a Full Fire

3

荡料入帘
Swinging into the Curtain

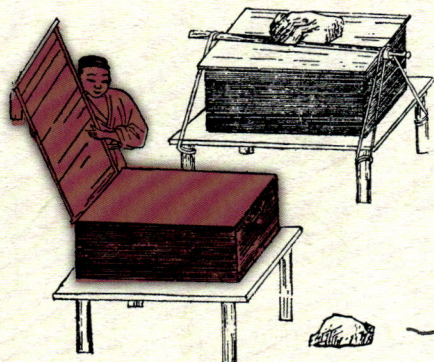

4

覆帘压纸
Covering Paper

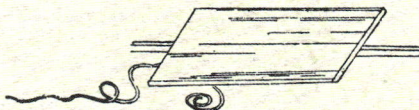

5

透火焙干
Drying Thoroughly

《天工开物》造纸工艺流程图
Paper Flow Chart in *Tiangong Kaiwu*

11. | 形形色色的纸
All Kinds of Paper

　　纸自诞生之日起，在千百年间得到了广泛应用，并逐渐被赋予了丰富多彩的表现形式，无论功用还是艺术性都有了很大的发展。比如，多用于宫廷殿堂写宜春帖诗词的洒金纸、被徐熙等著名画家用于作画的澄心堂纸等。

　　洒金纸起源于唐代，是加工纸中的高贵品种，纸表面粘有细碎金片或银片，光彩鲜艳夺目。金银箔的密度和成色越高则越名贵，造价也越高。洒金纸也可用作书画年卷引首、室内屏风，或用于委任文武官员的告身、少数民族政权首领的任命和录用文书等。

Since its birth, paper has been widely used for thousands of years. It has gradually been given a variety of forms of expression, and both its function and artistry have developed greatly. For instance, the gold applied paper (Gold-Flecked Paper) used in palace halls to write poems in Yichun Tie, Chengxintang paper used for painting by famous painters such as Xu Xi. Gold applied paper(Gold-Flecked Paper), originated in the Tang Dynasty, is a noble variety in processed paper. The paper is covered with tiny flakes of gold or silver, which are dazzlingly bright. The higher the density and fineness of the gold and silver foil, the more expensive it is and the higher the fabrication cost. Gold applied paper can also be used as the preface of the scroll, interior screen, or for the appointment of civil and military officials, the appointment and employment of the heads of ethnic minority regimes, and so on.

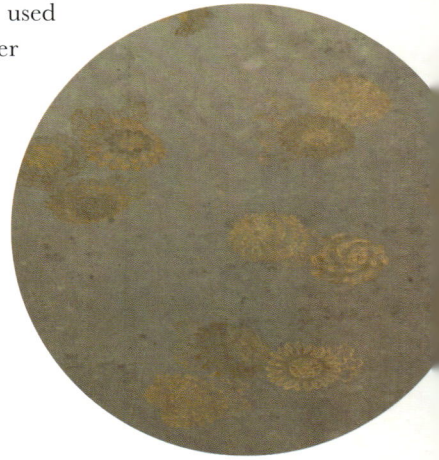

明宣德仿五代澄心堂纸
Cheng xin tang Paper, Ming Daynasty

洒金纸
Gold Applied Paper
(Gold-Flecked Paper)

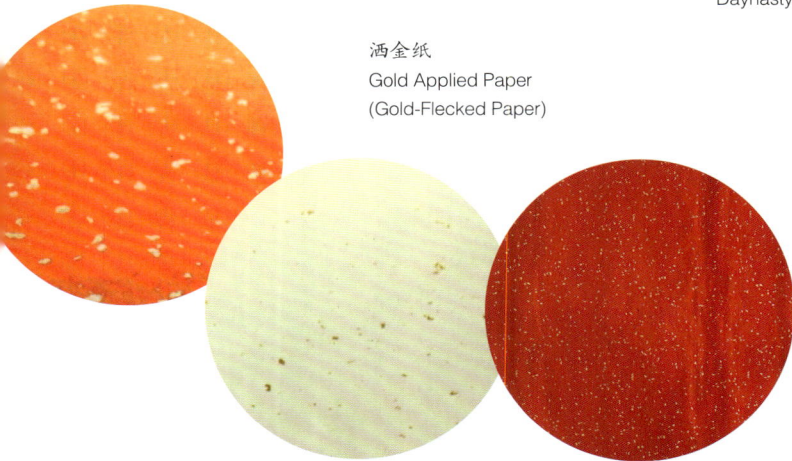

金粟山藏经纸
JinSu Mountain Sutra Paper

12. 印刷术出现之前的技术准备
Technical Preparation before Printing Technology

在雕版印刷术产生之前，我国古代有两种文字和图案复制方法——捺印和拓印。

捺印是将雕刻在印章上的文字或图案钤盖在纸上的方法。早在先秦时期就出现了印章，捺印技术由此产生。用来钤盖印章的捺印，初期主要盖在封泥上，用作个人凭信。唐贞观年间从印度传来的佛像捺印技术才更近似雕版印刷工艺。

拓印约起源于南北朝，兴盛于隋代，是一种将各种器物的凹凸图文或碑刻文字用纸、墨捶印出来，以便保存和传播的工艺方法。这种以正写阴文复制正写文字的方法为雕版印刷术的发明提供了极为宝贵的经验。

Rubbing and sealing are two important methods of copying text and patterns in ancient China before the production of block printing.

Sealing is a method of covering texts or patterns engraved on a stamp on paper. As early as the pre-Qin period, the stamp had appeared, and sealing techniques had then been produced. The sealing used to cover the stamp was originally placed on the sealing mud and used as a personal pledge. The Sealing technique of the Buddha statues from India in the Zhenguan period of the Tang Dynasty was more similar to the block printing techniques.

Rubbing is originated from the Northern and Southern Dynasties and flourished in the Sui Dynasty. It is a process that prints, reserves and spreads the concave and convex images or stone inscriptions on various artifacts with paper and ink. This method of copying the text written in the negative text provided an invaluable experience for the invention of block printing.

苏州石刻天文图拓片
Suzhou Stone Carving
Astronomical Map Rubbings

13. 雕版印刷术
Block Printing

公元7世纪（隋末唐初），中国人受印章和拓印技术的启发在而发明了雕版印刷术。雕版印刷术是将文字或图像反刻在木板或其他材质上，然后敷墨刷印到纸张上的技术。

早期的雕版印刷术多用于印刷佛经、佛像、历书等，五代时开始用于印刷儒家经典。到宋代，雕版印刷发展到鼎盛时期。直到清代后期，随着近代西方印刷机械的传入，雕版印刷才逐渐被取代。

雕版印刷术发明后不久就传播到朝鲜、日本和越南等国，随后传到中亚、西亚和北非，并于14世纪传到欧洲。印刷术成为人类文化的共同财富，有力地促进了社会文明的发展。

Inspired by seals and inscription rubbing techniques, the Chinese invented the block printing in the seventh century AD (Late Sui and early Tang Dynasty). Block printing is a technique for engraving text or images on wood or other materials and then applying ink to the paper.

Early block printing was mostly used to print Buddhist scriptures, statues, almanacs, etc. In the Five Dynasties, it began to be used to print Confucian classics. In the Song Dynasty, block printing reached its heyday. Until the late Qing Dynasty, block printing was gradually replaced with the introduction of modern Western machine printing technology.

Shortly after the invention of the block printing, it spread to Korea, Japan and other places, and then to Central Asia, West Asia and North Africa. Later it spread to Europe in the 14th century. Printing has become the commonwealth of human culture and has effectively promoted the process of social civilization.

刻刀：雕版工具
Graver: Engraving tool

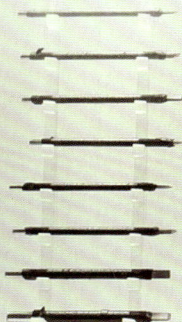

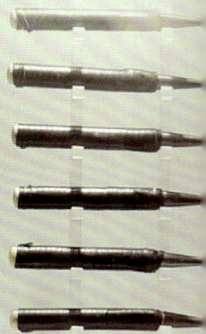

棕刷：刷印工具
Coir Brush: Printing tool

14. 雕版印刷术高度发达的产物——纸币
A Highly Developed Product of Block Printing—Paper Money

中国是世界上最早发明纸币的国家。早在北宋时期，四川地区印刷发行了世界最早的纸币——交子。南宋时，朝廷在都城临安（今杭州）设立"行在会子务"，大量发行纸币"会子"。后来，又发行了"关子"以取代"会子"。元代纸币制度更加完善，元政府发行了全国通行的纸币——宝钞。历代纸币大多用金属或硬木雕版印刷而成，并采用了多色套印技术。

元朝时期，纸币传到印度、波斯和欧洲，对各地货币制度产生了重大影响，至今纸币仍是世界各国普遍使用的货币形式。

China was the first country to invent paper money. As early as the Northern Song Dynasty, the Sichuan area printed the world's first paper money — Jiaozi. In the Southern Song Dynasty, the imperial court set up "the office of issuing Huizi" in the capital, Lin'an (now Hangzhou) and issued a large number of paper money "Huizi". Later, "Guanzi" was issued to replace "Huizi". The paper currency system of the Yuan Dynasty was improved. The Yuan government issued Paper Money of Yuan. Paper money of the past dynasties was mostly printed in metal or hardwood blocks, and Multi-Color printing technology was adopted.

During the Yuan Dynasty, paper money spread to India, Persia and Europe, exerting a great influence on the monetary system of various parts of the world. Till date, paper money is still the form of currency commonly used in countries around the world.

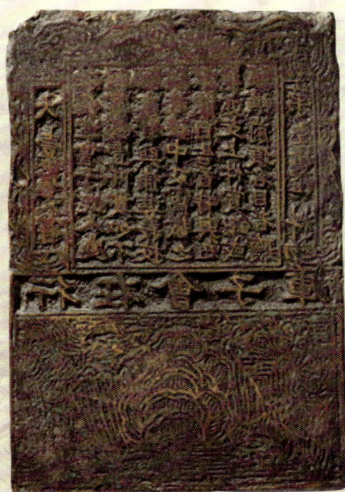

南宋"行在会子库"铜版及印刷品
Copperplate of "Issued Huizi", Southern Song Dynasty

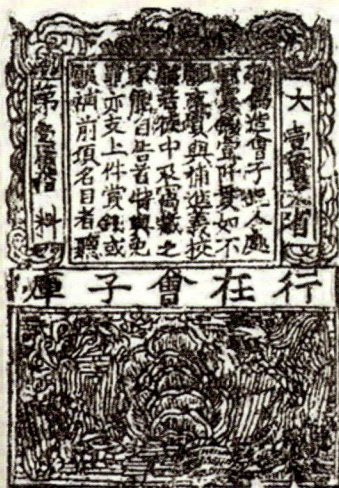

元"至元通行宝钞"铜版
Copperplate of "Issued Paper Money of Yuan", Yuan Dynasty

15. 印刷史上的一次革命——活字印刷术的发明

A Revolution in Printing History—The Invention of Typography

　　北宋庆历年间（1041—1048），工匠毕昇发明了活字印刷术。他用胶泥制作成形如印章的活字，每字一印，烧制成陶。排版时在铁模里放上松香、蜡、纸灰等的混合物，上面摆满活字，以火加热后将其压平，待冷却后便可印刷。印完后将活字取出，以备下次再用。为提高效率，他还同时设置两块铁板，交替排版与印刷，高效快捷。

　　活字印刷术的发明克服了雕版印刷费工、费时、费力以及雕版存放不便等缺点，大大提高了工作效率，是印刷史上的一次重大革命。大约14世纪，活字印刷术通过丝绸之路传到欧洲。受其启发，德国人谷登堡发明了铅活字印刷术。

During the Qingli Years of the Northern Song Dynasty (1041—1048), the craftsman Bi Sheng invented typography. He made movable-type characters in the shape of the seal, printing each word and firing it into pottery. While typesetting, a mixture of rosin, wax, paper, ashes, etc. is placed in an iron mold, covered with movable type, which is pressed flat after heating and then allowed to be printed after cooling. After printing, the movable type can be taken out for later use. To improve efficiency, he also set up two iron plates at the same time, alternating typesetting and printing. Thus it would be quite efficient and fast.

The invention of typography overcame the disadvantages of block printing, such as time-consuming and laborious work and inconvenient storage. Since it greatly improved the working efficiency, it was a significant revolution in printing history. Through the Silk Road, typography spread to Europe around the 14th century. Inspired by this, the German Gutenberg invented lead type printing.

毕昇
Bi Sheng

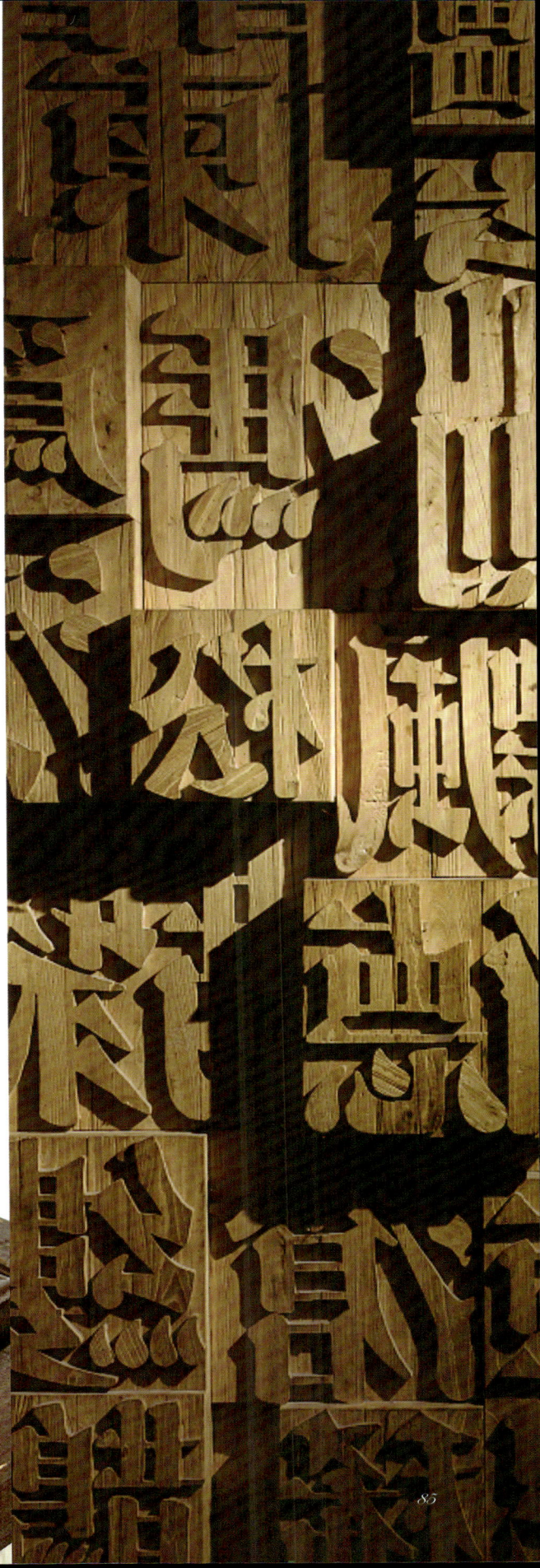

16. 木活字印刷术与转轮排字盘

Wood Type Printing and Typesetting Turnable

　　木活字印刷出现于南宋时期，其方法是在木板上刻好阳文反字之后锯成一个个单字字模，将字模排列在木框内，用小竹片塞紧后涂墨铺纸刷印。

　　到了元代，一位名叫王桢的农学家改进了木活字印刷术。他发明了用于存放木活字的工具——转轮排字盘。排字盘由两个大圆盘组成，字盘直径为七尺、高三尺，有竖轴可以转动。字盘上分为若干格，用于排放活字，一盘上的活字按韵序存放，另一盘存放"杂字"。排版时，一人读稿并指出韵号，另一人推动转盘取字。以字就人，既高效又快捷，是排字技术上的一个创举。

Wood type printing appeared in the Southern Song Dynasty. The method is to engrave the positive characters on a wooden board and then saw them into monograms. Arrange the type molds in the wooden frame, and tighten it with small bamboo pieces, then apply ink and cover the paper on it for printing.

In the Yuan Dynasty, Wang Zhen, an agronomist, improved wood type printing. He invented Typesetting Turnable, a tool for storing wood movable types. The Typesetting Turnable is composed of two large disks, with seven feet in diameter and three feet in height, and a vertical axis for rotation. It is divided into several cases for the discharge of movable type. The movable characters on one plate are stored according to the rhyme and the miscellaneous characters on the other. During typesetting, one person reads the manuscript and points out the rhyme, while the other runs the wheel to take out types. Being efficient and fast, it is a pioneering work in typesetting technology.

转轮排字盘复原模型
Restoration Model of Wheel
Typesetting Plate

17. 瓷器从何处来
Where Does Porcelain Come From

瓷器由陶器发展而来，它是古人通过原料选择、釉料配方、窑炉结构设计等长期实践的成果。

制瓷所需瓷土有瓷石和高岭土。瓷石中含有各种矿物岩石，制出的瓷器透明度和光泽均良好。高岭土是一种非金属矿产，色白而细腻，具有良好的可塑性和耐火性。釉料配制主要通过控制釉料中不同金属元素比例而使瓷器的釉色丰富多彩，釉面机械强度高，抗腐蚀能力强。窑炉的结构设计以南方的龙窑、北方的馒头窑、景德镇蛋壳窑为典型代表。

Porcelain is developed from pottery. It is the result of long-term practice by the ancients through raw material selection, glaze formula, and kiln structure design.

The clay of porcelain is mainly composed of porcelain stone and Kaolin. Porcelain stone contains various mineral rocks, and the porcelains produced are of good transparency and gloss. White and delicate, Kaolin is a non-metallic mineral with good plasticity and fire resistance. The glaze of porcelain is rich in color. And different colors are made up of different metal proportions in the glaze through Glaze preparation. The glaze has high mechanical strength and strong chemical resistance. The structural design of the kiln is represented by the dragon kiln in the south, the bread kiln in the north, and the eggshell kiln in Jingdezhen.

瓷坯
Glazed Pottery

瓷石
Porcelain Stone

高岭土
Kaolin

釉料
Glaze

18. 制瓷工艺流程
Porcelain Process

　　瓷器是中国人的伟大发明。制瓷工艺非常复杂，需要经历取土、练泥、制坯、画坯、荡釉、烧窑、开窑、彩器、炉烧等多道工序。

　　根据清代《陶冶图》记载，一件官窑青花瓷器从选料到成品要经历二十几道工序，即采石制泥、淘练泥土、炼灰配釉、制造匣钵、圆器修模、圆器拉坯、琢器做坯、采取青料、拣选青料、印坯乳料、圆器青花、制画琢器、蘸釉吹釉、旋坯挖足、成坯入窑、烧坯开窑、圆琢洋彩、明炉暗炉、束草装桶、祀神酬愿等。此二十几道工序已属简化后的概述，若依《天工开物》中的记载，瓷器的制作甚至多达72道工序。

Porcelain is a great invention of the Chinese. The porcelain-making process is very complicated, and it needs to go through multiple processes such as soil extraction, mud training, blank making, blank drawing, glazing, kiln firing, kiln opening, coloring, furnace firing and other processes.

According to the records in *Taoye Tu* of the Qing Dynasty, a piece of official kiln blue and white porcelain has to go through more than 20 processes, from materials selection to the finished product. That is, quarrying stone and making mud, washing and scouring soil, making ash and glaze, making saggers. Round ware repairing and throwing, hollow ware drawing blank, picking and selecting cobalt blue pigment, printing blank and milk material, blue and white round ware, drawing and cutting ware, dipping and blowing glaze, jiggering and digging. Put the billet into the kiln and firing, imitate Western techniques and draw colorful pictures on round and hollow ware. Put them into the open and closed furnace. Then wrap with grass and put them into the bucket. In the end, offer sacrifices to gods and reward gods etc. This 20-step procedure is really a simplified overview. According to the records in *Tiangong Kaiwn*, there are even 72 processes during the production of porcelain.

展项装置：观众通过观看拉洋片的方式，了解瓷器制作的工艺流程
Exhibition:The visitor can know the flow chart of procelain making process by displaying Layang films

练泥

镀坯

荡釉

开窑

制瓷工艺流程图
Procelain Process

19. 宋元名瓷
Porcelains From the Song and Yuan Dynasties

宋、元时代是中国瓷器制造的辉煌时期。无论是器型设计还是釉料创新，宋元瓷器一直都是后来者模仿的榜样。

受文人士大夫审美取向的影响，宋代瓷器融入了"文人气质"。闻名后世的汝、官、哥、钧、定五大名窑瓷器的器型朴素大方，釉色典雅高贵，把中国瓷器带入了新的美学境界。

元代，在继承前代制瓷技艺的基础之上发明了青花、釉里红等新的瓷器品种，并进一步融合中国绘画技巧，推动釉下彩瓷器进入新的发展阶段。

The Song and Yuan Dynasties were the glorious periods of Chinese porcelain manufacturing. Whether it is the design of the vessel or the innovation of the glaze, the porcelain of the Song and Yuan dynasties has always been a model for latecomers to imitate.

元青花釉里红瓷——拼图玩具
Blue and White,Glazed Red Porcelain,Yuan Dynasty — Jigsaw Puzzle

Deeply influenced by the aesthetic orientation of literati, the porcelain of the Song Dynasty mingled a lot with the "literati temperament". There were five world-renowned kilns: Ru Kiln, Jun Kiln, Guan Kiln, Ge Kiln and Ding Kiln. Their simple and elegant shape and elegant glaze bring Chinese porcelain into a new aesthetic realm.

By inheriting and developing from the porcelain of the previous generation, new porcelain varieties such as blue and white, and glazed red appeared in the Yuan Dynasty. They further integrated Chinese painting techniques and promoted Chinese underglaze color porcelain into a new stage of development.

陶瓷坊展项全景
Panoramic View of Ceramic Workshop

20. 陶器上的文化交流——唐三彩
Cultural Exchange on Pottery—Tri-Colored Glazed Tang Wares

　　唐三彩是唐代为适应厚葬之风而创制的一种低温釉陶器。它名曰"三彩"，其实是一种多彩釉陶器，釉色包含绿、蓝、黄、白、赭、褐等多种色彩，只要陶器具备两种以上的颜色便可统称为"三彩"。

　　唐三彩凭借着一流的釉料配制工艺和高超的塑形技术，迅速成为中国陶瓷宝库中的珍品，同时借助唐代强大的文化辐射力，通过丝绸之路传到世界各地，也是为宋代以后的低温釉和釉上彩的发展打下了坚实的基础。

As low-temperature glazed pottery, Tri-colored Glazed Tang Wares was invented and prevailed in the Tang Dynasty in line with the custom of the elaborate funeral. Tricolor, as it is called, is a kind of multi-glazed pottery. Glaze colors include green, blue, yellow, white, ochre, brown and other colors. As long as pottery has more than two colors, it can be collectively referred to as tricolor.

With its first-class glaze preparation technology and superb shaping technology, Tri-colored Glazed Tang Wares has quickly become the jewel of the Chinese Ceramic Technology. It also spread to the rest of the world through the Silk Road with the powerful cultural radiation of the Great Tang Dynasty. Meanwhile, it laid a solid foundation for the development of low-temperature glaze and overglaze color after the Song Dynasty.

三彩马
Horse of Tri-Colored Glazed Tang Wares

三彩骆驼人俑
Camel-Carrying-Figurines of Tri-Colored Glazed Tang Wares

21. 瓷器上的文化交融——青花瓷

Cultural Exchange on Porcelain — Blue and White Porcelain

　　青花瓷最早出现在唐代，元代以后渐趋成熟。它以白地蓝花或蓝地白花为风格特征，蓝白两色对映，朴素明快，爽朗大方。它的烧制工艺是先以钴料为呈色剂在瓷坯上彩绘，然后罩上一层透明釉，一次入窑烧制而成。从元代开始，青花瓷便远销海外，享誉世界。

　　青花瓷的工艺发展及纹饰演变生动地反映了中外技术与文化的交流。青花瓷的氧化钴着色技术源自西亚。元青花及明永乐、宣德青花瓷所用的钴料苏麻离青从波斯进口。青花瓷的造型与纹饰在外销过程中也受到当地艺术风格的影响。青花瓷烧造技术通过阿拉伯人传到欧洲后，对欧洲蓝彩软质瓷器的出现起到了巨大的推动作用。

Blue and white porcelain first appeared in the Tang Dynasty, and gradually became mature after the Yuan Dynasty. It is characterized by white ground blue flowers or blue ground white flowers. The color is simple and clear. The blue and white reflect each other, bright and elegant. It's painted on a porcelain slab with cobalt as a coloring agent and then covered with a layer of transparent glaze. Firing the porcelain slab in the cellar once, then we could get blue and white porcelain. Since the Yuan Dynasty, blue and white porcelain has been exported to overseas and has gained a worldwide reputation.

The development of technology and decorative patterns of blue and white porcelain reflect the exchange of technology and culture between China and foreign countries. The cobalt oxide coloring technology was introduced to China from West Asia. The cobalt material Smaltum(Su Ma Liqing) used in blue and white porcelain of the Yuan Dynasty, Yongle and Xuande of the Ming Dynasty was imported from Persia. With the export trade, its shape and decorative patterns also absorbed and learned a lot from the local artistic style. The firing technology of blue and white porcelain spread to Europe through the Arabs and played a great role in the emergence of soft-paste blue porcelain.

互动青花纹饰投影装置：观众转动盘子便可以变换出不同历史时期的青花瓷纹饰
Interaction with Blue and White Projector Device: By rotating the plates, the visitor can view different decorative patterns of the blue and white porcelain in different dynasties

22. 以瓷为媒的商贸和技术交流
Trade and Technology Exchange with Porcelain as the Medium

　　瓷器是中国享誉世界的伟大发明，它通过海上和陆上丝绸之路销往世界各地。至明清时期，中国向西方出口的瓷器达1.5亿件以上，形成了瓷器出口贸易的高潮。中国的制瓷技术也随之传到海外，推动了日本、朝鲜及中东、欧洲等地制瓷业的发展，在世界范围内产生了巨大影响。

　　中国制造的外销瓷在融入外销地多元文化的同时，也实现了自我艺术的突破。

Porcelain is a great creation of China with a world-famous reputation. Chinese porcelain has been sold to the rest of the world through the sea and land silk roads. During the Ming and Qing Dynasties, China exported at least 150 million pieces of porcelain to the West, forming a climax of porcelain export trade. China's porcelain-making technology was also spread overseas, promoting the development of porcelain-making industries in Japan, Korea, the Middle East, Europe and other places. There has been a huge impact worldwide.

China's exported porcelain has not only integrated into the multi-culture of the export market but also achieved a breakthrough in its own art.

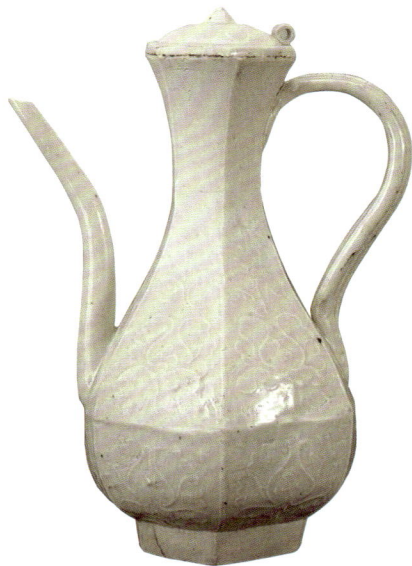

"南海1号"出水瓷：宋德化窑青白釉六棱印花执壶（文物）
Porcelain Excavated from Ship "Nanhai No.1": Bluish-white-glazed hexagon ewer with stamped pattern (Cultural Relic) Dehua Kiln, Song Dynasty

"南海1号"出水瓷：宋德化窑青白釉印花盘（文物）
Porcelain Excavated from Ship "Nanhai No.1": Bluish-white-glazed floral-mouth plate with stamped pattern (Cultural Relic) Dehua Kiln, Song Dynasty

23. 中国水利机械
China Water Conservancy Machinery

中国古代水利机械出现早、应用广。先秦时已经出现了杠杆式的提水工具——桔槔。汉代的提水工具进一步发展，发明了灌溉机械——翻车，并出现了利用水力推动的碓和磨等粮食加工工具。东汉时发明了水力驱动皮囊鼓风的冶铁水排。东晋出现了连机水碓，即用水轮带动多个碓同时工作。宋元时期，水利机械的使用更加成熟和普遍。各地修建了很多筒车，利用河流自动提水灌溉。有的粮食加工作坊用一个水轮同时驱动磨、砻、碾工作，成为联合加工作坊。

Ancient Chinese water conservancy machinery appeared very early and was widely used. In the pre-Qin period, a lever-type water lifting tool "Jiegao" appeared. In the Han Dynasty, the water-lifting tools were further developed, and the irrigation machinery-chain pump was invented. And there were water-powered tools for processing grain such as hoes and mills. In the Eastern Han Dynasty, the smelting iron platoons were invented to drive the leather bags blast by hydraulic power. There was a machine called "Serial tilt hammer" in the Eastern Jin Dynasty, in which the water wheel drove multiple water hammers to work at the same time. During the Song and Yuan Dynasties, the use of water conservancy machinery was more mature and common. Many bucket wheels were built in various places to take advantage of the river and automatically irrigate. Some food processing workshops use a water wheel to drive, smash and grind at the same time, becoming a joint workshop.

提水灌溉类 / Water Irrigation Tools

手摇翻车 /Hand-Cranked Rollover

手摇翻车又称拔车，依靠手摇车拐带动大齿轮转动，从而将水由低处运到高处。

Hand-cranked rollover is also called pulling car. It relies on a hand-cranked component to drive the big gear to rotate, thus transporting water from low to high.

脚踏翻车 / Foot-Cranked Rollover

脚踏翻车是在大齿轮轴的两端安装脚踏板，人脚踩动踏板就可驱动大齿轮和木链轮转。

The pedal type rollover is to install foot pedals at both ends of the large gear shaft. When people step on the foot pedals, the large gear and the wooden sprocket can be driver to rotate.

筒车 / Truck

筒车是将很多竹、木水筒安装在水轮上，利用水流推动水轮将水筒提升到高处，其中的水自动倾倒出来，多用于农业灌溉。

The truck is equipped with a lot of bamboo and wooden water buckets on the water wheel. Using the momentum of the water flow, the water bucket is raised to a high position. Then the water inside is tilted out automatically and used for agricultural irrigation.

黄河大水车 / Yellow River Waterwheel

黄河大水车是一种利用水流自然冲击力的提水灌溉工具，丰水期利用自然水流推动，枯水期则以围堰分流聚水，通过堰间小渠聚水推动。

The Yellow River Waterwheel is a water conservancy facility that utilizes the natural impact of the Yellow River current. The waterwheel stands on the south bank of the Yellow River. The natural water flow is used to promote the rotation during the busy season. In dry season it divides the water by the cofferdam to finally gather water together to be self-propelled.

水磨 /Water Mill

水磨一般使用卧式水轮，利用水流冲击水轮，驱动石磨。

Water mill generally uses a horizontal water wheel, which uses the water flow to drive the stone mill.

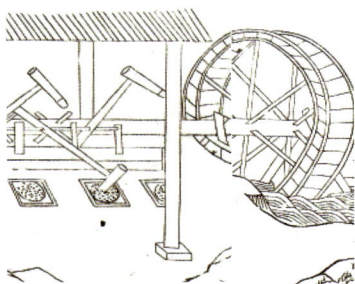

连机水碓 / Serial Tilt Hammer

连机水碓是用传动机构将多个碓联动起来，用一个水轮来驱动。采用立式水轮，轮径较大。

The machine is connected with a plurality of water pipes by a transmission mechanism, and driven by a water wheel. The water wheel adopts a vertical water wheel with a large wheel diameter.

船磨 / Ship Grinding

船磨是将石磨安放在船上，船固定在水面上，用立式水轮驱动石磨。

Ship grinding is to place the stone grinder on the ship. The ship is fixed on the water surface and the stone grinder is driven by a vertical water wheel.

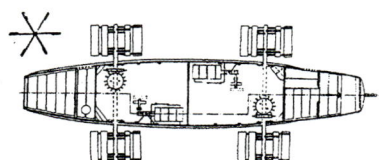

冶铁水排 /The Smelting Iron Platoons

冶铁水排用水轮驱动鼓风器，为冶铁炉鼓风，冶炼生铁。它可有效节约人力成本，有助于扩大炉容，增加产能。

The smelting iron platoon uses the water wheel to drive the air blower, blasting air into the iron furnace to smelt pig iron. It effectively saves labor cost, helps to expand furnace capacity and increases production capacity.

24. 外国水利机械
Foreign Water Conservancy Machinery

　　世界不同国家、不同民族都发明了以水为工作介质的水利机械。在古埃及和亚述时期，已经用杠杆原理提水灌溉。古希腊时期出现了著名的阿基米德抽水机。在古罗马时代，被称为"波斯轮"的畜力提水机械已经在使用。古罗马人将卧轴下冲式水轮与水斗组合为戽斗车，利用流水提水灌溉。这时期还出现了引山溪驱动水轮的原始水磨。6世纪，船磨的发明实现了无论河水涨落，水磨都可以正常运转。自11世纪起，很多作坊开始以水轮作为原动机，完成浆洗、鼓风、锻打、锯木等工作，这有力地推动了手工业的发展。

Different countries and nations in the world all invented their own water conservancy machinery, taking water as a working medium. In ancient Egypt and Assyria, levers were already used for irrigation according to the leverage principle. The famous Archimedes pumping machine appeared in ancient Greece. In the ancient Roman era, the animal-power-cranked lifting machine known as the Persian Wheel has already been used. In ancient Rome, the horizontal shaft water wheel was combined with the water bucket to form the bucket wheel for irrigation (powered by flowing water). During this period, the original watermill that led the mountain stream to drive the water wheel also appeared. In the 6th century, ship grinding appeared, with water either rising or falling, the watermill was able to operate normally. Since the 11th century, many workshops used the water wheel as the prime power, and completed the work of washing, blasting, forging and sawing, etc. It effectively promoted the development of the handicraft industry.

阿基米德抽水机 / Archimedes Pumping Machine

它是阿基米德螺旋线的实际应用，螺杆每转一周，密封腔将水向前推进一个螺距，随着螺杆的连续转动，水便提升了上来。

The Archimedes pumping machine is a practical application of the Archimedes spiral. Every time the screw rotates, the sealed cavity pushes the water forward by a pitch. With the continuous rotation of the screw, the water rises up.

波斯轮 / Persian Wheel

波斯轮是利用牲畜来驱动齿轮组，使用立式水轮，用水罐将水提升至高处，从侧方倾倒。

The Persian wheel uses livestock to drive the gear set, using vertical tank wheels to lift the water and pour it from the side.

庌斗车 / Bucket Truck

庌斗车是将很多水斗安装在水轮上，水轮为卧轴下冲式，利用水流的冲力将水斗提升到高处，再倾倒出来，多用于农业灌溉。

The bucket truck is equipped with a lot of water buckets on the water wheel. The water wheel is under the horizontal axis and can lift the water bucket to higher places using the power of the flowing water, then tilting water out for agricultural irrigation.

船磨 / Ship Grinding

　　船磨是将船只固定在河面上，在两船之间安装下冲式水轮，驱动磨盘运转。无论河水涨落，船磨都可以正常运转。

The ship grinding is to fix the vessel on the river surface, and install a lower flushing water wheel between the two ships to drive the water mill for operation. No matter the river rises or falls, the water mill can still operate normally.

水力作坊 / Hydraulic Workshop

　　意大利的铁匠作坊中用下冲式水轮驱动卧轴转动，带动铁锤锻打铁器，同时带动两个鼓风器加热铁器。

Hydraulic workshop: In the Italian blacksmith shop, the horizontal axis is driven by the undershooting water wheel to drive the iron forging hammer, and the two air blowers are used to heat the iron.

海上历险

Maritime Adventure

远洋船运具有运载量大、运输成本低的优势，往往成为丝路商旅运输大宗货物的首选。但海面浪大风疾，天气阴晴不定，给安全航行带来挑战。来自世界不同地区的工匠与水手发明了船只在海上导航定位的方法，并取长补短、吐故纳新，一道在大洋上搏击风浪，开启了大航海时代的序篇。

　　"海上历险"展区通过对航海与造船知识的展示，观众可以了解到海上丝绸之路上东西方海船船型、建造方法，以及船舶属具工作原理、海上导航、测时、测速等方法，最后通过气势恢宏的古代远洋船队模型，感受古人征服海洋、拥抱世界的胸怀。

With the advantages of large carrying capacity and low transportation cost, ocean shipping was often the first choice for merchants along the Silk Road to transport bulk goods. However, the sea was rough and windy, and the weather was changeable, which brought challenges to safe navigation. Craftsmen and sailors from different parts of the world explored and invented ways to build strong ships to navigate and locate at sea, learning from each other's strengths. They fight against the wind and waves on the ocean together, opening the preface of the era of great navigation.

Through the exhibition of navigation and shipbuilding knowledge in the "Maritime Adventure" exhibition area, the visitor can understand the ship types, construction methods, working principles of ship accessories, maritime navigation, time measurement, speed measurement and other methods of sea ships in the East and the West on the Maritime Silk Road. Finally, through the magnificent ancient ocean fleet model, the visitor can feel the ancient people's mind of conquering the ocean and embracing the world.

1. 船型——中西方古船船型差异
Ship Structures—Differences between Chinese and Western Ancient Ship Structures

　　自古以来，船舶就是重要的水上交通工具。在15—19世纪，船舶是海上交通的唯一载体。15世纪的海上探险，16—17世纪的地理大发现，18—19世纪的海上争霸和海外移民，都与船舶密切相关。世界船舶史是人类文明史和科技史的一个缩影。

　　曾有人对中西方的古代船只进行比较研究，中国古代船型大都具有一个基本特征，即船型的最宽处在中部靠后的地方。而西方船只的最宽处在中部靠前的地方，或者在纵向中轴线的正中处。为什么会有这种差异呢？西方人是这么说的："因为我们最好的船体是用鱼来做模型的，向头的一端常常比较大。但是中国人却模仿蹼足水鸟，它们浮水的时候，把最宽的部分放在后面。在这方面，他们是精明的，因为水鸟像船一样，是浮在空气与水的两种介质之间，而鱼却只能在水里游泳。"欧洲人认为他们应当按照鱼的外形来造船，而中国人却认为应当按照水鸟的外形来造船。事实证明，中国古船不但最宽处一般在中部靠后的地方，而且有些船型就是用鸟来命名的，甚至在船头画上鸟的图形。

Since ancient times, ships have been an essential means of water transportation. In the 15th-19th centuries, ships were the only carriers of maritime transport. Maritime expeditions in the 15th century, geographical discoveries in the 16th and 17th centuries, and naval supremacy and overseas immigration in the 18th and 19th centuries were all closely related to ships. The history of world ships is a microcosm of the history of human civilization, science and technology.

They found that although there are many kinds of ships in ancient China, most of them share one primary feature, the widest part of the ship lies is in the back middle part of the ship, not in the front centre part or the centre of the longitudinal centre axis like the western ships. Why is there such a difference? Westerners say this: "Because our best ship body is modelled with fish, the end of the head is often large. But the Chinese imitate the waterfowl, and when they float, they put the widest part behind. In this respect, they are very wise, because waterfowl is like a ship, floating between two media, air and water, while fish can only swim in the water." Europeans think they should follow the fish's shape to build the ship, but the Chinese believe that the ship should be made according to the body of the waterfowl. It turns out that the ancient Chinese ships not only put the widest part in the back middle, but some of the ships were named after the birds, and even the figures of the birds were painted on the bow.

中国福船
Fu Ship

阿拉伯三角帆船
Arabian Dhow Ship

中国古代四大海船 / Four Ancient Chinese Sea Ships

沙船 / Sand Ship

　　起源于唐代（618—907），是一种大型运输船只，因其可在水浅多沙的航道上航行而得名。沙船方头方尾，甲板宽敞，容积大，船舷较低。船体采用大梁拱，能够在强风大浪中快速前进。沙船的桅杆和帆很多，航行速度快，舵的面积大且能够升降，可抗击七级风浪，适航性强。

Originated in the Tang Dynasty (618—907), it is a large-scale transport vessel, named for its ability to navigate on the shallow and sandy waterway. The sand boat has a square head and a square tail, a spacious deck, a large volume and a low side. The hull adopts girder arch, which can move forward rapidly in strong wind and waves. It has many masts and sails, fast sailing speed, large rudder area and can be lifted and lowered. It can resist seven wind waves and has strong seaworthiness.

鸟船 / Bird Ship

　　起源于宋代（960—1279），分布于浙江沿海一带，因其船首形似鸟嘴而得名。鸟船头小身肥，船身长直，船头尖细，设有桅、蓬（帆），两侧有橹，有风扬帆，无风摇橹，行驶快速灵活。

It originated in the Song Dynasty (960—1279) and was distributed along the coast of Zhejiang Province. It was named after its bow-shaped like a bird's beak. The bird ship has a small and fat bow, a long straight body and a slender bow. It is equipped with masts and sails. There are oars on both sides. The sails can be hoisted in the wind, and the oars can be used flexibly without wind.

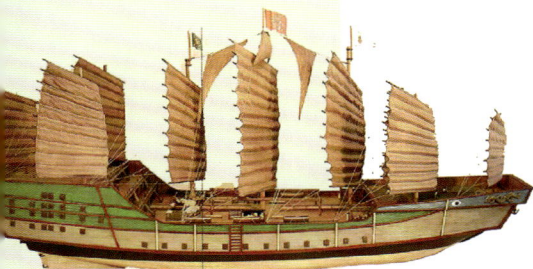

福船 / Fu Ship

　　出现于宋代（960—1279），流行于福建、浙江沿海地区的一种尖底海船。福船可吃水4米，以行驶于南洋和远海著称。福船高大如楼，底尖上阔，首尾高昂，两侧有护板，甲板平坦，龙骨厚实，已采用水密隔舱技术，安全性能优越。

It is a kind of pointed bottom sea ship that appeared in the Song Dynasty (960—1279) and is popular in the coastal areas of Fujian and Zhejiang. Fu ship can have a draft of four meters and is suitable for the sea voyage. Fu ship is as tall as a building, with a wide bottom tip, high head and tail, protective plates on both sides, flat deck and thick keel. It has adopted watertight compartment technology and superior safety performance.

广船 / Guang Ship

　　产于广东，是我国古代南海航线的一种重要船型。它的基本特点是头尖体长，吃水比较深，梁拱小，甲板脊弧不高。船体的横向结构由紧密的肋骨和隔舱板构成，纵向强度依靠龙骨和大橝维持。广船结构坚固，有较好的适航性能和续航能力。

Produced in Guangdong, it is a vital ship type in the South China Sea Route in ancient China. Its primary characteristics are long head and body, deep draft, small beam arch and low deck ridge arc. The transverse structure of the hull is composed of tight ribs and bulkhead plates, and the keel and Lie maintain the longitudinal strength. The construction of the ship is stable and has good seaworthiness and endurance.

其他地区的代表性船型 / Representative Ship Structures around the World

柯克船 / Kirk Ship

　　柯克船起源于北欧，原为小货船，其特点是船体短而宽，结构坚固，使用矩形横帆作为主要推进动力。13世纪起随着货运量的增长，它也相应地加大了尺寸。从14世纪起，它逐步成为英国的主要船型，最大的柯克船载重量可达400～500吨。到15世纪，其船体建造方法由搭接改为了平接，材料也开始使用橡木，为船型的进一步增大创造了条件，使其在许多欧洲国家得以推广。

Kirk ship originated in northern Europe and was originally a small cargo ship. It is characterized by the short and wide hull, firm structure, and the use of rectangular sail as the main propulsion power. Since the 13th century, with the growth of freight volume, it has also increased the size accordingly. Since the 14th century, it has gradually become the primary ship type in Britain, and the largest Kirk ship has a carrying capacity of 400—500 tons. In the 15th century, the method of hull construction was changed from lap joint to flat joint, and oak was also used as the material, which created conditions for the further expansion of ship type and promoted it in many European countries.

地中海桨帆船 / Mediterranean Sailboat

　　地中海"加莱型"桨帆船是一种窄长、低矮而灵活的以划桨为基本推进手段的船型。它的船体宽度较窄、型深较浅、干舷较低，所以稳定性和适航性较差。虽然它也配备了帆，但主要是在长途航行时使用，作用是让桨手们节省体力。从腓尼基和古希腊开始，历经古罗马帝国、拜占庭等时期，前后总共约3000年，它在地中海历史上的诸国争霸中扮演了一个非常重要的角色。

The Mediterranean "Calais" sailboat is a kind of narrow, long, low and flexible ship type, which takes rowing as the primary propulsion means. Due to the narrow width, shallow depth and low freeboard, the stability and seaworthiness of the ship are poor. The sail on the ship is mainly used for long-distance sailing and saving the rowers' physical strength. From Phoenicia and Greece, through the Roman Empire, Byzantine and other periods, a total of about 3000 years, mediterranean sailboat played a significant role in the struggle for supremacy in the Mediterranean history.

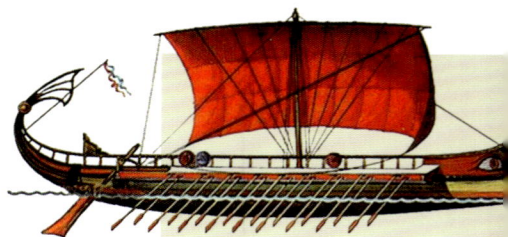

维京船 / Viking Ship

在人们的印象中，维京船就等于是北欧海盗船，同时也被用作商船，在斯堪的纳维亚地区从事海上贸易，活跃于8—11世纪。维京船的船首通常用一个龙头雕像作为标志，船体十分修长，使用搭接法建造。维京船有四大特点：（1）单桅挂方形软帆；（2）无甲板也无舱壁；（3）船员坐在船舱里划桨；（4）无舵，尾部设操纵桨。由于维京船船身修长，长度达到10～30米，所以也被称为"长船"。高高的曲线型两端及较深的舯部吃水使其具有良好的船舶操纵性。

In people's impression, the Viking ship, active from the 8th century to the 11th century, is equivalent to the pirates ship, also used as a merchant ship, engaged in maritime trade in Scandinavia. The bow of a Viking ship is usually marked by a statue of a dragon's head. The hull is very slender and is built by lapping. There are four characteristics of Viking ships: (1) single mast with square soft sail; (2) no deck or bulkhead; (3) crew rowing in the cabin; (4) no rudder and control oar at the stern. Due to the slender body of the Viking ship, the length reaches 10—30 meters, so it is also known as the "longship". The high curved ends and deep midship draught make it have good manoeuvrability.

阿拉伯三角帆船 / Arabian Dhow Ship

阿拉伯帆船分布在阿拉伯湾、红海及印度洋沿岸，通常为独桅或双桅，船首尖削，首柱高耸。早期的阿拉伯帆船使用操纵桨和梯形横帆，9—12世纪过渡到了使用船尾转轴舵和斜三角帆。

This ship was distributed in the Arabian Gulf, red sea and Indian Ocean coastal countries, usually single mast or twin mast, with a pointed bow and towering bows. From the 9th century to the 12th century, the Arabian sailing boats in the early Arabian sailing ships used the steering oars and trapezoidal sail. They completed the transition from the use of the stern pivot rudder and the oblique, triangular sail.

2. 船帆——不同样式的风帆

Sails—Different Styles of Wind Sails

船帆是人类的重要发明，自从有了船帆，人类才有可能利用自然界取之不尽、用之不竭的风力实现驰骋海洋的梦想。人类在利用风帆航行中创造了各式风帆：欧洲帆船最早流行矩形（或梯形）横帆，阿拉伯帆船流行三角帆，而中国帆则形成了撑条式平衡纵帆的独特式样。中国帆的帆幕上装有平行的竹制撑条，有助于保持帆面平整，可以根据风力大小和航行需要来分级收缩帆面积。

与欧洲的横帆相比，阿拉伯的三角帆迎风航行的性能更出色，但是，这种帆的操作极其耗费人力。中式风帆位于桅杆前面的平衡面积占总面积的大约1/6～1/3，加上独特的缭绳系统，操作简便，转动自如，通过调节帆的角度，使船只可以适应不同风向，有利于逆风航行。

The sail is an essential human invention. Since the sails have been made, human beings can take advantage of nature's inexhaustible wind to realize the dream of galloping in the ocean. Humans created a variety of wind sails in the practice of sailing. In the beginning, rectangular or trapezoidal formed sails were famous in Europe, while triangle ones were popular in Arab. The Chinese sail was unique because of its superiority. In the long-term practice, the Chinese sail has formed a unique style of "strut-type balanced vertical sail". This kind of sail is equipped with parallel bamboo bracing on the sail screen, which helps to keep the sail flat. The sail area can be reduced according to the wind force and navigation requirements.

Compared with the horizontal sails in Europe, the windward performance of the triangle sails is better, but the operation of this kind of sail is exceptionally labour-intensive. The balance area of the Chinese style sail in front of the mast accounts for about 1/6—1/3 of the total size. The unique rope winding system is easy to operate. By adjusting the angle of the sail, the ship can adapt to different wind directions, which is conducive to sailing against the wind.

阿拉伯的三角帆
Rectangular Sail

风
K
I
J
H
G
F
E
D
B
C
A

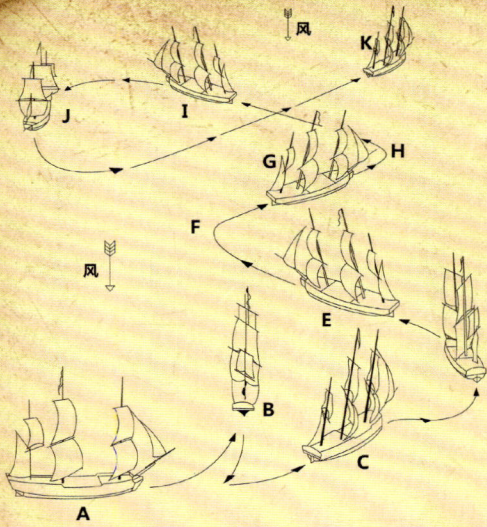

船帆在逆风条件下航行原理图
Schematic Diagram of Sail Sailing in
Upwind Condition

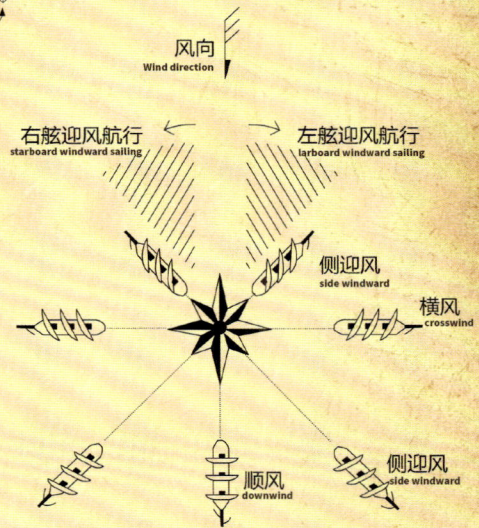

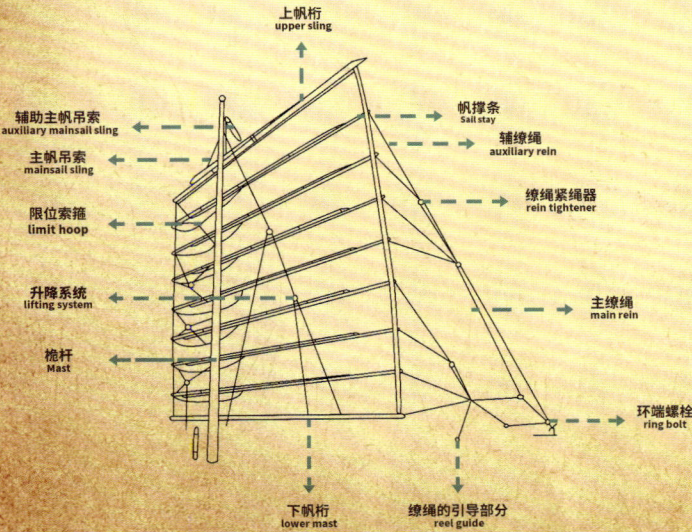

风向
Wind direction

右舷迎风航行
starboard windward sailing

左舷迎风航行
larboard windward sailing

侧迎风
side windward

横风
crosswind

顺风
downwind

侧迎风
side windward

上帆桁
upper sling

辅助主帆吊索
auxiliary mainsail sling

主帆吊索
mainsail sling

限位索箍
limit hoop

升降系统
lifting system

桅杆
Mast

帆撑条
Sail stay

辅缭绳
auxiliary rein

缭绳紧绳器
rein tightener

主缭绳
main rein

环端螺栓
ring bolt

下帆桁
lower mast

缭绳的引导部分
reel guide

中式风帆——撑条式平衡纵
帆结构图
Structural Drawing of Chinese
Style Sail—Braced Balanced
Longitudinal Sail

3. 船舵
Rudder

　　舵是用以改变和保持船舶航行方向的设备，安装于船的尾部，一般由舵柄、舵杆和舵叶三部分组成，均用硬质木材制成。舵的工作原理就是当船航行时，船尾水流在舵面上形成水压——舵压。舵压虽然小，但由于它与船的重心距离比较大，所以使船转动的力矩也比较大。根据杠杆原理，舵压推动船转动的效果就很显著。

　　舵是由中国人在东汉时期发明的。中国人在使用舵的过程中不断改进和创新，先后发明了升降舵、平衡舵和开孔舵。

　　舵的使用和发展使远洋航行成为可能，船尾舵传到西方后对地理大发现和文明进步做出了巨大的贡献。

The rudder is a device used to change and maintain the navigation direction of the ship. When the ship is sailing, the water generated by the stern forms a water pressure on the rudder surface—the rudder pressure. Although the rudder pressure is minimal because it has a relatively large distance from the centre of gravity of the ship, the torque for turning the ship is relatively large. According to the principle of the lever, the effect of propelling the ship is powerful.

The rudder was invented by the Chinese in the Eastern Han Dynasty. In the process of using the rudder, the Chinese have made continuous improvement and innovation, and successively invented lifting rudder, balance rudder and perforated rudder.

The use and development of rudder made the ocean voyage possible. The stern rudder made an outstanding contribution to the tremendous geographical discovery and the development of civilization.

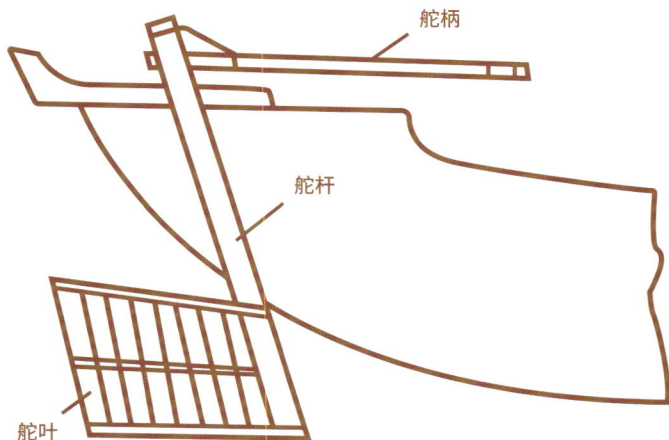

舵柄

舵杆

舵叶

舵装置结构图
Structure Diagram of Rudder Device

拖舵：1955年在广州东郊的东汉墓中出土了一艘陶船模型，其尾部有控制航向的拖舵

Dragging Rudder : In 1955, a model of a pottery vessel was unearthed from the Tomb of the Eastern Han Dynasty in the eastern suburbs of Guangzhou. Its stern had a dragging rudder to control the heading direction

《清明上河图》中绘制的船舶：全部使用平衡舵，也就是把一部分舵面安排在舵轴的前面，从而减少转舵力矩，使得操舵较为省力

The Ships Drawn in *Riverside Scene at Qingming Festival* : All used spindled rudders, they were all balance rudders too, that is, a part of the rudder surface is placed in front of the rudder axle, thereby reducing the steering torque and making the steering less laborious

升降舵：根据水的深浅可以随时调节舵的高低

Lifting Rudder: The height of the rudder can be adjusted at any time according to the depth of the water

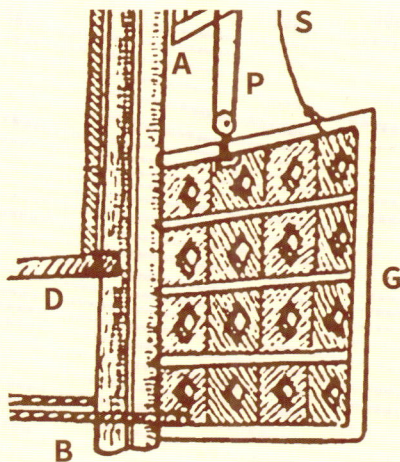

开孔舵：舵叶两侧的水是相通的，可以使转舵力矩有所减小，一般也不影响舵效

Perforated Rudder: The water on both sides of the rudder blade is connected,which can reduce the rudder moment and generally does not affect the rudder effect

4. 船体建造技术——阿拉伯三角帆船
Hull Construction Technology—Arabian Dhow Ship

马可·波罗时代，在印度洋沿岸地区普遍使用一种叫作"Dhow"的阿拉伯三角帆船，船壳板构件都用椰树纤维捻制的绳索绑扎在一起，并在拼缝侧面用敷料来保证船体不漏水。

阿拉伯三角帆船采用"船壳优先"建造法。缝合建造时，船体先以龙骨为中心组装船壳成形，等船壳完成后再安装肋骨和横梁等结构。由于绑扎的绳索寿命短，阿拉伯三角帆船每隔几年必须重新绑扎。

In Marco Polo's time, in the coastal areas of the Indian Ocean, one type of ship named "dhow" was widely used. The hull plates were all tied together with ropes made of coconut fibre, and the side of the seam was covered with dressings to ensure that the hull was watertight.

The "hull first" construction method is adopted for Arabian dhows. During the construction, the hull is assembled with the keel as the centre, then the frame and beam are installed on the hull. Due to the short life of the Arabesque, the jib has to be lashed every few years again.

阿拉伯帆船船体连接结构模型

Hull Connection Structure Model of Arabian Dhow Ship

5. 船体建造技术——中国帆船

Hull Construction Technology—Chinese Sailing Ship

　　中国帆船采用"骨架优先"建造法。建造时，先把横向隔舱壁安装在龙骨上，再以龙骨、首尾柱和隔舱壁形成的骨架为基础来进行船壳板的安装。这种造船方法有利于木船向大型化方向发展。

　　中国帆船木料选用软硬适中的杉木、松木，船壳板为双层，木材的连接依靠榫卯结构并用铁钉加固，再以桐油、石灰、麻絮捻缝。船底舱用横向隔舱壁隔开，以增强船体抗击侧向水压、风浪的能力。船底涂漆，不仅能减少水的阻力，还能防止浸腐而保护船体。

The "skeleton first" construction method is adopted for Chinese sailing ship. During construction, the transverse bulkhead is first installed on the keel, then the hull plate is installed based on the framework formed by the keel, fore and aft columns and bulkhead. This shipbuilding method is conducive to the development of large-scale wooden ships.

Chinese sailboats are made of fir and pine wood with moderate hardness and softness. The hull plate is double layered. The wood is connected by mortise and tenon structure and reinforced with iron nails, and then caulked with tung oil, lime and flax floc. The bottom cabin of the ship is separated by transverse bulkhead to enhance the hull for resisting the lateral water pressure and wind waves. Bottom painting can reduce the resistance of water, prevent corrosion and protect the hull.

中国帆船船体结构模型
Hull Structure Model of Chinese Sailing Ship

蛇头同口
Snake head tenon joint

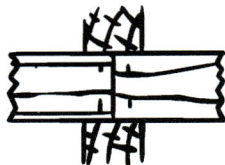

平面同口
Plane tenon joint

滑间同口
Sliding room tenon joint

直角同口
Right angle tenon joint

咬合同口
Holding-on tenon joint

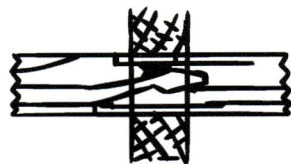

鱼尾同口
Fish tail tenon joint

斜面同口
Bevel tenon joint

钩子同口
Hook tenon joint

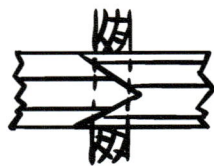

叉子同口
Fork tenon joint

中国帆船木材榫接方式
Mortise and Tenon Used in Chinese Sailing Ship

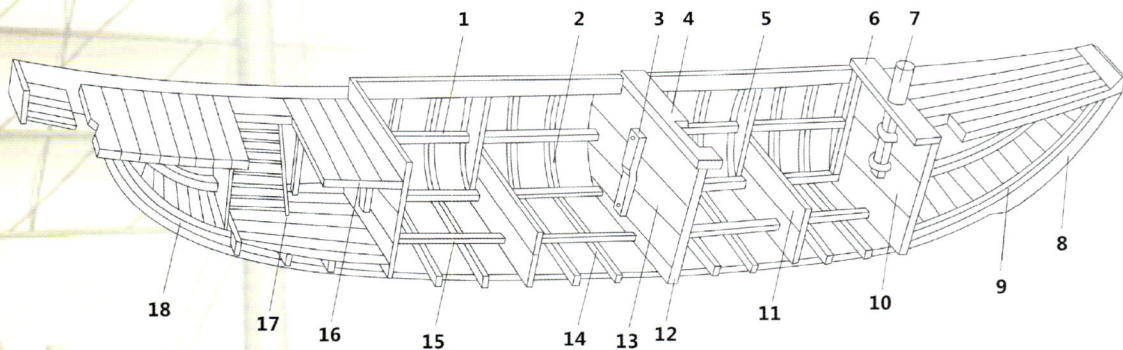

中国帆船船体结构图：1.边压筋；2.肋骨；3.舱壁扶强材；4.桅面梁；5.肘梁；6.面梁；7.首系缆桩；8.首护筋；9.首压筋；10.隔舱板；11.半隔舱板；12.桅脚梁；13.桅满梁；14.脚梁；15.底亚筋；16.托梁；17.立柱；18.尾压筋。
Structural Drawing of Chinese Yacht Sailing Ship：1. Side stiffener; 2. Frame; 3. Bulkhead stiffener; 4. Mast face beam; 5. Elbow beam; 6. Surface beam; 7. Bow bollard; 8. Head guard bar; 9. Head stiffener; 10. Bulkhead; 11. Semi bulkhead; 12. Mast foot beam; 13. Mast full beam; 14. Foot beam; 15. Bottom sub reinforcement; 16. Joist; 17. Column; 18. Tail bar

6. 船体建造技术——水密隔舱
The Hull Construction Technology—Watertight Compartment

　　中国人大约在晋代发明了水密隔舱，其主要组成部分是水密隔舱壁，这些舱壁把船体沿纵向分割成一个个不连通的舱室。水密隔舱的首要功用是提升船体安全性：如果某个舱破裂或者漏水，由于舱壁的阻隔，其他舱不受影响，船舶可以继续安全航行。其次，横向隔舱板还有力地支撑船的两舷，使得船体能够抵抗水的压力并具备抵御风浪的能力。此外，船舱分区也有利于船上货物和供应品进行分类存放，便于装卸和管理。水密隔舱的发明是中国人模仿大自然的杰作。西方学者认为，中国人发明水密舱壁是借鉴了竹子的横隔膜结构。由于古代欧洲没有竹子，因此欧洲人无法获得这方面的灵感。

The Chinese invented the watertight compartment around the Jin Dynasty. Its main components are watertight bulkheads, which divide the hull longitudinally into disconnected compartments. The primary function of the watertight compartment is to ensure that the hull has strong, safety precations: if a compartment is broken or leaks, the other compartments, blocked by the bulkhead, will not be affected, and the ship can continue to sail safely. Secondly, the lateral bulkheads also support the ship's sides, making the hull resistant to water pressure and wind and waves. In addition, the cabin division is also conducive to the classification and storage of cargo and supplies on board, which is convenient for loading, unloading and cargo management. The watertight compartment invention is a masterpiece of the Chinese imitating nature. Western scholars believe that the Chinese invented the watertight bulkheads by borrowing the diaphragm of the bamboo. As there was no bamboo in ancient Europe, Europeans did not have this inspiration.

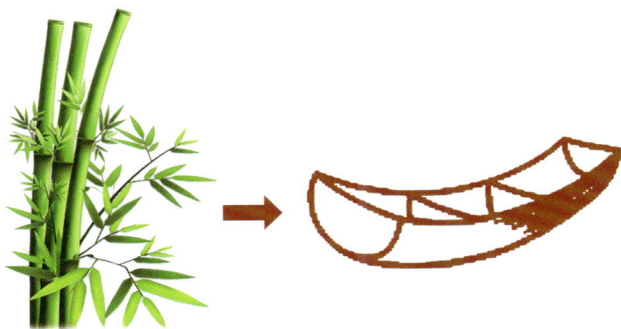

从竹子的横隔膜结构到水密隔舱
From the Diaphragm of the Bamboo to Watertight Compartment

水密隔舱剖面模型
Watertight Compartment Profile Model

7. 地文导航——灯塔
Geographic Navigation—Lighthouse

亚历山大灯塔——古埃及 / 亚历山大城
Lighthouse of Alexandria—Ancient Egypt / Alexandria

始建于公元前280—前278年，高120米，建立在巨大的方形底座上，中部是八角形的建筑，上部是直径稍小的圆柱体建筑。灯设在顶部，以树脂为燃料，用大型金属镜面聚光，据说56千米外都能看到。亚历山大灯塔是古代世界七大奇迹之一。

It was first built in 280—278 BC, with a height of 120 meters. The Lighthouse is on a vast square base with an octagonal building in the middle and a cylindrical building with a slightly smaller diameter in the upper part. The light is located at the top, using resin as fuel, and a large metal mirror as the spotlight, which is said to be visible 56 kilometres away. Alexander lighthouse is one of the seven wonders of the ancient world.

意大利热那亚灯笼塔——意大利 / 热那亚城
Genoa Lantern Tower—Italy / Genoa City

始建于12世纪前期，修建在圣贝尼尼奥山丘上，为砖石结构，高76米，海拔117米，是热那亚的标志性建筑。

The construction started in the early 12th century, and the tower was built on the hills of San Benigno. It is a masonry structure with a height of 76 meters and located at an altitude of 117 meters. It is the landmark of Genoa.

科尔杜昂灯塔——法国 / 科尔杜昂
Corduone Lighthouse—France / Corduone

始建于1584年，位于吉伦特河口处。科尔杜昂灯塔是法国现存最古老的灯塔，最早建于岩石上，被海浪拍打。

The Corduone Lighthouse, built in 1584 at the mouth of the Gironde, is the oldest existing lighthouse in France. It was first built on rocks and beaten by the waves.

广州怀圣寺光塔——中国 / 广州
Guangzhou Huaisheng Temple Light Tower—China/Guangzhou

始建于唐贞观年间（627—649），塔高30多米，为青砖砌筑，外抹灰沙，光洁如柱。唐代时，夜晚塔顶悬灯，为过往船只导航，故称"光塔"。

It was built in zhenguan year of the Tang Dynasty (627—649). The light tower is more than 30 meters high. It is made of blue bricks and is covered with grey sand, looks very clean and neat. In the Tang Dynasty, lights were hung on the top of the tower at night to guide passing ships, so it was called "light tower".

泉州六胜塔——中国 / 泉州
Quanzhou Liusheng Tower—China/ Quanzhou

始建于北宋，元至元二年（1336）重建，为仿木结构的楼阁式建筑，八角五层，底围约46米，高约31米，浑体石砌。

Quanzhou Liusheng Tower was rebuilt in Zhiyuan Year of Yuan Dynasty. It is a wooden-like pavilion-style, five-story building with an octagon. The bottom perimeter of the stone tower is about 46 meters, and the height is 31 meters.

8. 地磁导航——指南针的发明
Geomagnetic Navigation—The Invention of Compass

先秦时期，中国人已经认识到磁石吸铁及指南的现象，并制成了最早的磁性指南工具——司南。司南由磁石打磨成的磁勺和方形青铜盘组成。将磁勺放于铜盘上，转动勺把，待静止时勺把指向南方。

中晚唐时期，中国发明了用铁与磁石摩擦磁化制作的指南针，并发现了地磁偏角。

北宋时期，指南针获得极大发展，发展出水浮、缕悬、指爪、碗唇等安置方式，还发明了用热剩磁磁化效应制作指南针的工艺。在此时期，中国人还率先将指南针用于航海导航。

In the pre-Qin period, Chinese people had discovered the phenomenon of magnet absorbing iron and guide, then made the earliest magnetic guide too—Sinan. Sinan is composed of a magnetic spoon and a square bronze plate. Place the spoon on the plate and turn the handle. When it is still, the handle points to the south.

In the middle and late Tang Dynasty, the compass made by iron magnetization was invented in China. At the same time the ancient Chinese people discovered the geomagnetic declination angle.

During the Northern Song Dynasty, the compass was greatly developed, the various methods such as water-floating, thread-suspension, finger-claw and bowl-lip were developed. The technology of making a compass with thermal remanence magnetization effect was also invented. In this period, the Chinese took the lead in using compass in navigation.

司南
Sinan

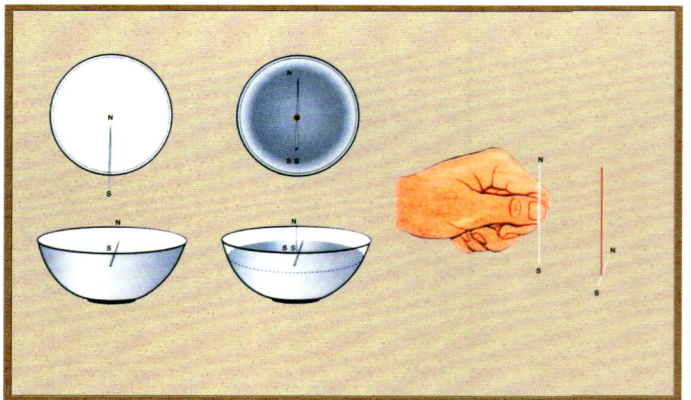

《梦溪笔谈》四种指南法示意图：北宋学者沈括于11世纪所著的《梦溪笔谈》记录了指南针的四种使用方法
Four Kinds of Guidelines in *MengXiBiTan*, Written in the 11th century by Shen Kuo, a scholar of the Northern Song Dynasty

水罗经：即水罗针，采用水浮法原理制作。木质水罗经以整木雕成，盘面周围刻二十四方位，内中盛水，磁针横穿灯芯草，浮于水面以指示方向

Water Compass : Also named water compass needle, which is made by the principle of water-floating method. The wooden water compass is carved from the whole wood, with 24 directions carved around the lip. With water inside the bowl, the magnetic needle crosses the cordyceps and floats on the water to indicate the direction

驾船游戏展品图：观众可以操纵船尾舵，通过多媒体游戏体验帆船驾驶

Sailing Game Exhibits：The visitors can control the rudder at the stern and experience sailing through multimedia games

9. 地磁导航——指南针的西传
Geomagnetic Navigation—The Westward Spread of Compass

　　欧洲人在古希腊时期已经发现了磁石吸铁等磁现象，但直到12世纪才开始使用磁罗盘。

　　阿拉伯人从公元13世纪开始在与中国的海上贸易中学会了使用指南针，他们的指南针是用鱼状铁片与磁石摩擦磁化而成，并将指南针放置在船尾用于导航。

　　指南针西传后，为欧洲日后的开辟新航路和地理大发现提供了必要的技术前提，极大地推动了各国航海业的发展，对中世纪以来的世界大融合产生了重要影响。指南针也被誉为影响世界的"四大发明"之一。

In ancient Greece, magnetism such as magnetite was discovered in the ancient Greek period, but it was not until the 12th century that the magnetic compass was used.

From the 13th century AD, the Arabs learned to use the compass in their maritime trade with China. Their compass was also magnetized by the friction of fish iron pieces and magnets, and the compass was placed at the stern for navigation.

After the compass was introduced to the West, it provided the necessary technical premise for Europe to open up new routes and geographical discoveries in the future. The compass also greatly promoted the development of the navigation industry in various places and had an important influence on the great integration of the world since the Middle Ages. The compass is also known as one of the "four great inventions" influencing the world.

13世纪阿拉伯水浮式指南针模型：水浮式指南针容易横向漂移，甚至接触罗盘壁，影响指向效果。13世纪阿拉伯文献记载的水浮式指南针用较长的磁铁片与木片交叉组合，有效地克服了这个缺点
Arabian Floating Compass Model in the 13th Century: The water floating compass is easy to drift laterally and cause friction with the direction plate, which affects the pointing effect. The water floated compass recorded in Arabic Literature in the 13th century effectively overcame this shortcoming by using a long cross combination of magnet and wood chips

航海罗盘模型：17世纪欧洲带有常平环的航海罗盘模型
Nautical Compass Model: A 17th century European navigational compass with a constant ring

10. 天文导航——牵星术

Astronomical Navigation—Star-Tracing Technology

　　牵星术是古代测量天体地平高度的一种方法。只要测量出天体的地平高度，就可以推算出观测者的地理纬度。

　　牵星板是测定天体高度的工具。一副牵星板共有12片，每片板代表一个角度。在测量时，一根绳子穿在板中心，板的下边缘与海天线相齐，绳子拉直靠近眼窝位置，板的上边缘与被测天体相齐。如果观测时牵星板的上边缘不能与所测天体相切，就需要换另一块板，直至相切为止。这时，人眼对这块板的张角就是天体的地平高度角。这个看似简单却十分巧妙的方法解决了船只在茫茫大海中航行时的定位问题。

The star-tracing technology is an ancient method of measuring the height of the celestial body. As long as the height of the celestial body is measured, the geographic latitude can be calculated.

The star-tracing board is the tool for measuring the height of the celestial body. There are 12 pieces in one set of star-tracing boards, each one representing an angle. While measuring, a rope is threaded through the board centre, and the lower edge of the board is aligned with the sea antenna. The rope is drawn close to the eye socket, and the upper edge of the board is aligned with the object being measured. If the upper edge of the star-tracing board cannot be tangent to the measured object when observing, the other plate needs to be replaced until it is tangent. At this time, the angle of the human eye to the board is the angle of the horizon of the celestial body. This seemingly simple but very clever method gives a good answer to the problem of ship positioning in the vast sea.

牵星板
The Star-Tracing Board

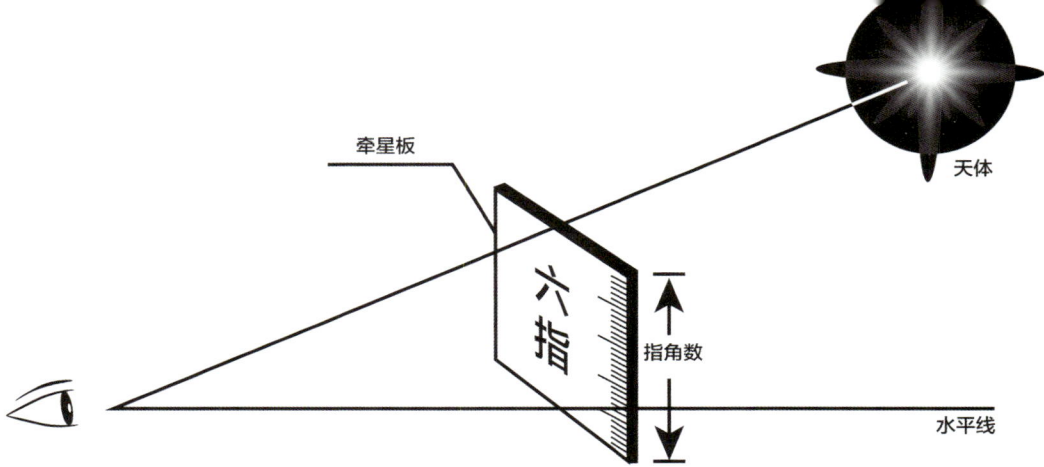

牵星板工作原理图

The Working Principle Diagram of the Star-Tracing Board

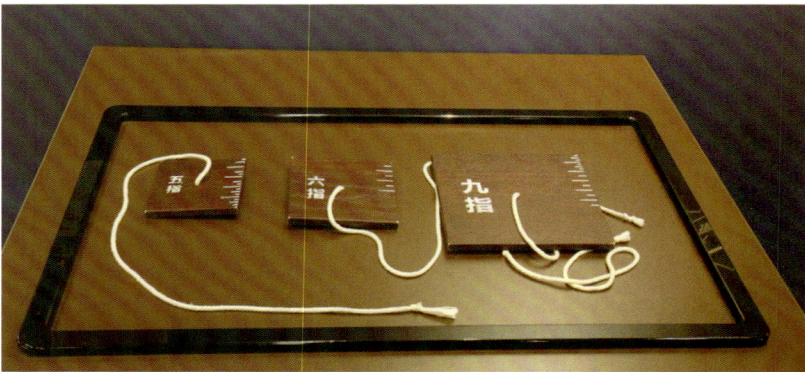

牵星板互动模型

Interaction Model of the Star-Tracing Board

牵星术：源自阿拉伯地区。古代阿拉伯人在航海中采用了类似牵星板的定位仪器。该仪器用9块板，第1块边长约为1小指长，1小指又分为4份，每份为1指，即第1块为4指，第9块为12指。观测者左手执板，右手执线，其基本原理与中国的牵星板相同

Start-Tracing Technology : Originated in the Arab region,and ancient Arabs used a positioning instrument similar to a star-tracing board in navigation. The instrument has 9 boards,the length of the first board is about 1 small finger length,and the 1 small finger is divided into 4 parts, each of which is 1 finger, that is, the first board has 4 fingers, and the 9 th board has 12 fingers. The observer's left hand holds the board and the right hand holds the line. The basic principle is the same as that of the Chinese star-tracing board

11. 天文导航——星盘
Celestial Navigation—Astrolabe

　　星盘是古代天文观测和航海使用的重要仪器，其起源可以追溯到希腊化时代或更早。它的用途非常广泛，包括定位和预测太阳、月亮、金星、火星等天体的位置，确定本地时间、经纬度和三角测距等。

　　星盘的主体是一个有圆周刻度的铜盘，在盘的正面有用球极平面射影法绘制的网络状星图和地平坐标网（在当纬度变化时要更换地平坐标网）。星图标有最亮的星和黄道，可以转动。地平坐标网有以天顶为中心的等高圈和方位角。

　　星盘在中世纪的阿拉伯和欧洲地区很流行，不仅成为基本的天文测量仪器，也被占星学家用作占星工具。

The astrolabe is an important instrument in ancient astronomy and navigation, and its origin can be traced back to the Hellenistic Age or even earlier. The astrolabe has a wide range of applications, including positioning and forecasting the position of the sun, moon, Venus, Mars and other celestial bodies, determining the local time and longitude and latitude, trigonometric ranging, etc.

The main body of the astrolabe is a copper disk with a circumferential scale. The reticular star map (Rete) and the horizon coordinate network (needs to be changed depending on the different latitudes) are painted in the front side of the disk using spherical plane projection method. The star icon has the brightest star and the ecliptic and can be rotated. The horizon coordinate network has contours and azimuths centered on the zenith.

The astrolabe became popular in the medieval Arab and European regions, not only becoming a basic astronomical measuring instrument, but also a divination tool for astrologers.

星盘：古代欧洲和阿拉伯世界测量天体高度的仪器
Astrolabe : An instrument to measure the height of a celestial body in ancient Europe and the Arabic world

12. 海上测速
Speed Measurement on the Sea

　　测量船速的方法有多种。最简单的方法就是根据船的已知长度，从船头向海上投掷一块木片，测量者随之向船后行走，并且始终与木片保持相同的水平位置，直到船尾，就可以测得行走时间，于是就可以计算出人行走的速度，也就得出了船相对于水的速度。

　　16世纪后期，欧洲开始用打结的绳子和沙漏来测定船速。两个绳结相隔7英寻（12.796米）。在测量时，先在船尾将绳子抛下。绳子一头绑着木板，木板下方有铅配重，让木板在水面上保持直立。等木板游离船尾后开始计时。船尾的人用沙漏计量时间。船员一边看着沙漏，一边从手中向后放绳子。半分钟沙漏漏完，手中过了5个节，航行的速度就是5。于是，"节"成了海船速度的计量单位。1节等于每小时行驶1.852千米。当今，国际上海水流速、海上风速、鱼雷等的速度计量单位也是"节"。

There are many ways to measure the speed of a ship. The easiest is to throw a piece of wood from the bow to the sea, and the measurer walks backwards to the end of the ship, maintaining the same horizontal distance from the piece. By measuring the walking time of the measurer, the speed of the ship can be estimated.

In the late 16th century, Europe began to use knotted ropes and hourglass to measure ship speed. The two knots are seven fathoms apart. During the measurement, the rope is first dropped at the stern. One end of the rope is tied to a board with a lead counterweight under it to keep it upright on the water. Wait until the planks free from the stern. The crew watched the hourglass and released the rope according to the speed of the ship. Half a minute hourglass, if the crew released five knots of rope, sailing speed is 5. As a result, "knots" became the unit of measurement of the speed of ships. One knot is equal to 1.852 kilometres per hour. In today's world, the speed measurement units of seawater velocity, sea wind speed and torpedo are also knots.

人行走的速度　＝　船航行的速度

Walking Speed　　　　　Sailing Speed

步行测速——追踪海面物品

Speed Measurement by Walking— Tracking Objects on the Sea

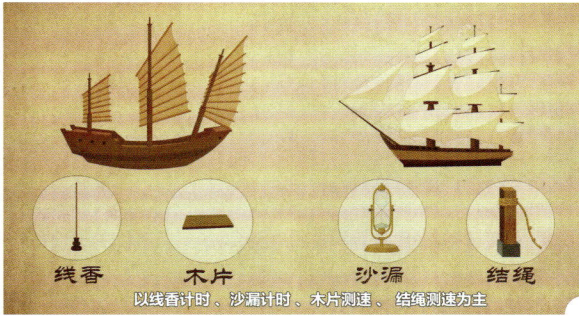

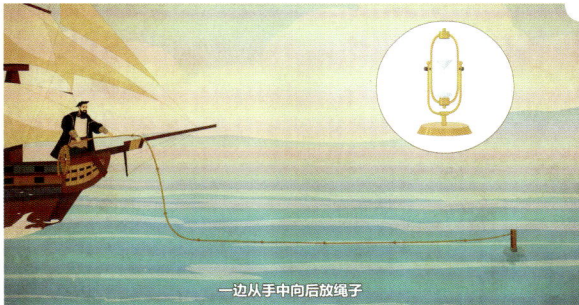

线香　　木片　　沙漏　　结绳

以线香计时、沙漏计时、木片测速、结绳测速为主

抛绳计节

虽然"抛绳计节"早已成为历史

一边从手中向后放绳子

航海的船员使用打结的绳子和沙漏来测定船速

工具测速：利用打结的绳子和沙漏

Tools for Speed Measurement : Knotted ropes and hourglass

13. 海上计时
Timekeeping on the Sea

中国古代航海计时法——线香 / Chinese Ancient Navigation Timing Method—Burning Incense

南朝梁时即有"烧香知夜漏，刻烛验更筹"之法。唐宋时期，航海以日为单位。大约自明代郑和航海起，将陆地上的点香计时方法移到航海上。燃香适用于颠簸的海上航行，也很容易测量时间。明代嘉靖年间的《筹海图编》记载："更者，每一昼夜分为十更，以焚香支数为度。"即将一昼夜均分为十更，则一更约合今 2.4 小时。

In the Liang Dynasty of the Southern Dynasties, there was the method of "burning incense to know the leakage of the night, and carving candle to test the watches of the night". In the Tang and Song Dynasties, the unit of navigation was day. Since Zheng He's voyage in the Ming Dynasty, the timing method of incense burning on land was transferred to navigation. Burning incense is very suitable for sailing in rough sea and easy to measure time. In the Jiajing period of the Ming Dynasty, *Chouhai Tubian* records that " one day and night is divided into ten watches, with the number of incense sticks as the degree." One watch is about 2.4 hours today.

将陆地上的点香计时方法转移到航海上

中国古代航海测量时间的工具——线香
Chinese Ancient Navigation Timing Method—Burning Incense

西方早期航海计时法——沙漏 / An Early Method of Maritime Timing in the West—Hourglass

　　西方早期航海也以"日"为单位，大约在12世纪，在指南针传入的同时，西方航海者开始用沙漏计时。从15世纪起，运行沙漏而为船舶的日志提供时间。沙漏也叫沙钟，是一种测量时间的装置。它是将两个玻璃球用一个细管连接起来。上面的玻璃球内充满沙子，穿过细管流入底部。一般的沙漏运行时间为1分钟。

In the early times of Western navigation, the unit of "day" was also taken as the unit. In the 12th century, when the compass was introduced, Western navigators began to use hourglass for timing. Since the 15th century, hourglass has been operated to provide time for ship logs. The hourglass, also known as sand clock, is a device for measuring time. It is to connect two glass balls with a thin tube. The glass ball above is filled with sand and flows through a small tube into the bottom. Generally, the running time of hourglass is 1 minute.

是一种测量时间的装置

西方古代航海测量时间的装置——沙漏
An Early Method of Maritime Timing in the West — Hourglass

14. 郑和下西洋
Zheng He's Voyages

1405—1433年，郑和率船队七下西洋，遍历南洋、印度洋诸国。西洋不是指现在的大西洋，而是指古代相对于中国的地理位置而言的西方大洋。

郑和七下西洋的前三次最远到达现在印度的卡利卡特，从第四次的航线开始逐渐延伸到现在的霍尔木兹、红海以及非洲东海岸。

郑和远航规模之大、航程之远、船舶之多、人员之众、所到地域之广在世界航海史上都是前所未有的，它加强了中外文化的交流，开了大航海时代的先河。

From 1405 to 1433, Zheng He led his fleet to "the west" seven times, travelling the southern and Indian Ocean countries. The "Western Ocean" does not refer to the present "Atlantic Ocean", but refers to the ancient Western Ocean relative to China's geographical location.

In Zheng He's seven voyages to the west, the first three times had reached kalikat, India; from the fourth voyage, the route gradually extended to Hormuz, the Red Sea and the east coast of Africa.

Zheng He's voyages are unprecedented in the history of navigation in terms of its large scale, long voyage, vast fleet, countless crews, and wide range of areas. Zheng He's voyages had strengthened the cultural exchange between China and foreign countries, and opened up a new era of navigation.

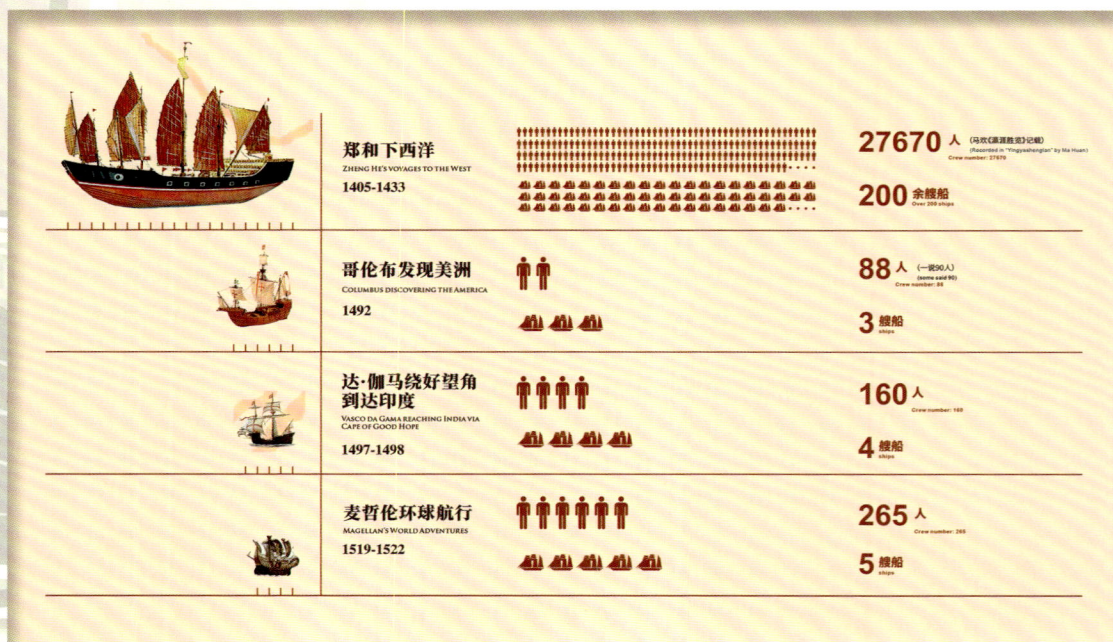

	郑和下西洋 ZHENG HE'S VOYAGES TO THE WEST 1405-1433		**27670** 人 (马欢《瀛涯胜览》记载) (Recorded in "Yingyashenglan" by Ma Huan) Crew number: 27670 **200** 余艘船 Over 200 ships
	哥伦布发现美洲 COLUMBUS DISCOVERING THE AMERICA 1492		**88** 人 一说90人 (some said 90) Crew number: 88 **3** 艘船 ships
	达·伽马绕好望角 到达印度 VASCO DA GAMA REACHING INDIA VIA CAPE OF GOOD HOPE 1497-1498		**160** 人 Crew number: 160 **4** 艘船 ships
	麦哲伦环球航行 MAGELLAN'S WORLD ADVENTURES 1519-1522		**265** 人 Crew number: 265 **5** 艘船 ships

世界历史上几次航海活动的规模比较
Comparison of Several Navigation Scales in World History

15. 郑和船队
Zheng He's Fleet

　　郑和船队约有各类大小船舶200余艘，是一支混合式联合船队，航行时的队形像一只飞燕，移动灵活，有利作战。船队在白天以旗帜为指挥讯号，晚上则以灯笼代替，如果遇到有雾、雨、雪等天气，便以锣、鼓、喇叭等乐器进行指挥和联络。

Zheng He's fleet has more than 200 ships of various sizes. It is a hybrid combined fleet. Its formation looks like a flying swallow when sailing, which is flexible and conducive to combat. During the day, the fleet uses flags(and lanterns at night) as the command signal. In case of fog, rain, snow and other weather conditions, the fleet will use gongs, drums, horns and other instruments to conduct command and communication.

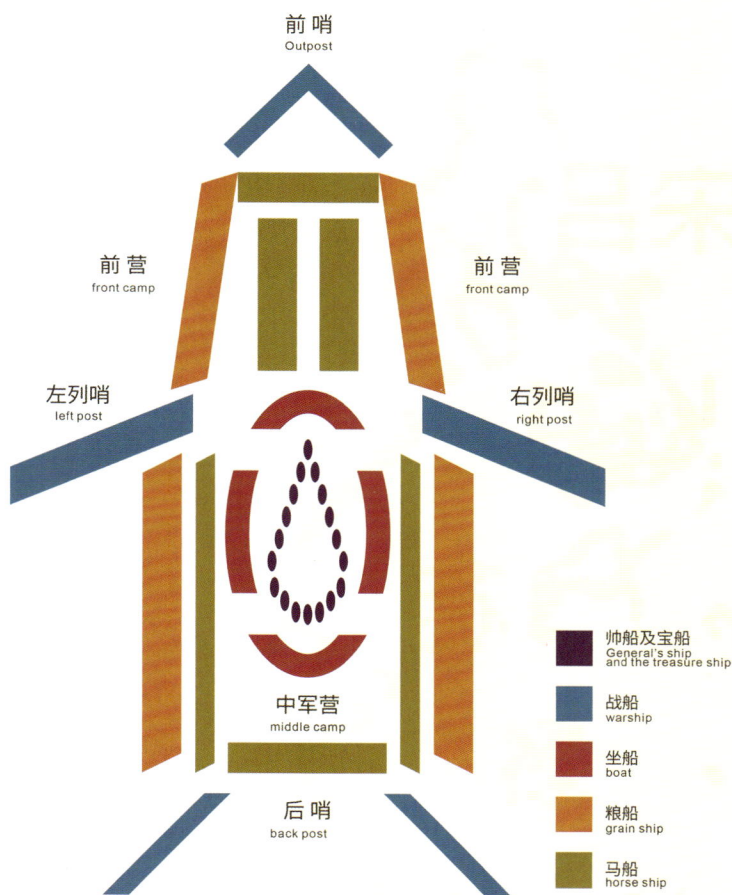

前哨
Outpost

前营
front camp

前营
front camp

左列哨
left post

右列哨
right post

帅船及宝船
General's ship
and the treasure ship

战船
warship

坐船
boat

粮船
grain ship

马船
horse ship

中军营
middle camp

后哨
back post

郑和船队编队示意图
Diagram of Zheng He's Fleet Formation

马船 / Horse Ship

　　大型快速水战与运输兼用船。

Large-scale fast combat and transportation vessel.

粮船 / Grain Ship

　　主要用于运输船队所需粮食及后勤供应物品。

It is mainly used to transport food and logistics supplies for the fleet.

宝船 / Treasure Ship

　　专门供船队的指挥人员、使团人员、外国使节乘坐，同时用来装运宝物。

It is specially for the commanders of the fleet, the members of the diplomatic corps the foreign envoys. It is also used for transporting treasures.

战船 / Warships

担任护航的专用船舶。

A special vessel serving as escort.

水船 / Water Ship

储存、运输淡水的专用船舶。

Special ships for storing and transporting fresh water.

坐船 / Zuo Ship

大型战船，又名"战坐船"。它是郑和船队中屯存水师、安营扎寨的主要船只。

Large warship, also known as "Zhan Zuo ship". It was the main vessel of Zheng He's fleet for storing navy crews and camping.

世界在变

The Changing World

汉语：你好

波斯语：Haló

土耳其语：Merhab

希腊语：Γεια

意大利语：ciao

哈萨克语：salam

阿拉伯语：السلام عليكم

英语：Hello

日语：こんにちは

印地语：namaste

俄语：Здравствуй

古老的丝绸之路在新时代焕发出新生机。古老造物在新兴科技的协助下绽放出新活力。科学领域的合作增进了人类对自然界的理解。源自丝绸之路交流的渴望，使信息与交通领域不断涌现创新成果，在文明之间架设起联通的桥梁。如果马可·波罗有机会踏上 21 世纪的丝绸之路，他定会为这些陌生而先进的科技感到惊奇，他也会欣慰地发现伟大的丝绸之路精神仍在传递。

在"世界在变"展区，观众穿越时空隧道回到现代，展览在此以闪回的方式呼应前五个展区出现过的展品，表现沿丝绸之路传播的古代科技对近现代科技的影响，体现东西方互学互鉴对于现代科技发展的作用，以及人人都能成为新时代"马可·波罗"的愿景。

The ancient Silk Road has gained new vitality in a new era. With the support of emerging technology, ancient creations are blossoming into new energy. Cooperation in science has improved man's understanding of the natural world. The desire for communication derived from the Silk Road has led to the constant emergence of innovative achievements in the field of information and transportation, building bridges between civilizations. If Marco Polo had the chance to set foot on the Silk Road of the 21st century, he would be amazed by these strange and advanced technologies, and he would be pleased to find that the great spirit of the Silk Road is still being transmitted.

In the exhibition area of "The Changing World", the visitor returns to the modern time through the space-time tunnel, and the exhibition echoes the exhibits in the first five exhibition areas in a flashback, showing the influence of ancient science and technology that spread along the Silk Road on modern science and technology. It reflects the role of mutual learning between the East and the West in the development of modern science and technology, and the vision that everyone can become the "Marco Polo" of the new era.

1. 青蒿素：传统中医献给世界的礼物

Artemisinin: A Gift From Traditional Chinese Medicine to the World

疟疾是全球重要的公共卫生问题之一，曾对人类健康造成重大危害。屠呦呦受东晋葛洪著《肘后备急方》中"青蒿一握，以水二升渍，绞取汁，尽服之"记载的启发，使用沸点较低的乙醚，通过低温萃取的方法，从植物黄花蒿中成功提取了青蒿素。经验证，青蒿素对疟原虫的抑制率达到100%，挽救了无数患者的生命。

凭借发现青蒿素，屠呦呦获得2015年诺贝尔生理学或医学奖。中医药这座蕴含着中华民族几千年智慧的宝库，正等待着我们运用创新之镐挖出造福人类的新宝藏。

Malaria is one of the most critical public health problems in the world, which has caused great harm to human health. In 1971, inspired by the record in *Handbook of Prescriptions for Emergencies* by Ge Hong in the Eastern Jin Dynasty which says "Soak a handful of artemisia Apiaceae herbs in two litres of water, press the mixture for its juice and drink it.", Tu Youyou and her team, with low-boiling-point ether, extracted successfully at low temperature from artemisia annua the artemisinin that 100% inhibits the plasmodium, which saved the lives of countless patients.

In 2015, Tu Youyou won the Nobel Prize in Physiology or Medicine for her achievement in the discovery of Artemisinin, which is the embodiment of the Silk Road spirit of integration of Chinese and Western medicine and mutual learning. Traditional Chinese medicine contains thousands of years of wisdom of the Chinese nation, waiting for us to use innovative minds to dig out new treasures for the benefit of mankind.

屠呦呦诺贝尔奖证书（复制品）
Tiu Youyou's Nobel Prize Certificate (Replica)

诺贝尔奖奖章（复制品）
Nobel Prize Medal (Replica)

展项：传统中医献给世界的礼物———青蒿素

Exhibit：A gift from traditional Chinese medicine to the world—Artemisinin

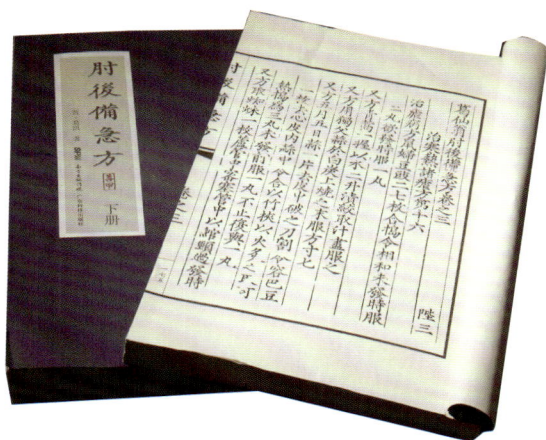

《肘后备急方》

Handbook of Prescriptions for Emergencies

2. 无处不在的玻璃
The Ubiquitous Glass

在古代，玻璃作为贵重的人造材料常用于装饰品和贵重容器的制作。玻璃器和玻璃制作工艺经丝绸之路广为传播。近代以来，玻璃的透光、折光、耐酸碱等特性被广泛应用，出现了透镜、棱镜、化学反应器皿等玻璃制品。这些玻璃制品推动了天文学、光学、生物学和化学的革命性进步，促成了近代科学的诞生。这些因玻璃而发生的科技成就又沿丝绸之路传至各地。如今，天文望远镜、显微镜、生化实验设备仍离不开玻璃组件。

在生产和生活领域，玻璃可谓无处不在。照明设备、建筑采光、电子设备屏幕、交通工具舷窗……处处都离不开各式特种玻璃。可以说，玻璃是现代世界的重要物质组成部分，它作为最重要的人造材料之一还会继续与人类社会的发展同行。

In ancient times, as valuable human-made material, glass was often used in the production of ornaments and valuable containers. Glassware and glassmaking techniques were widely spread along the silk road. Since modern times, the characteristics of light transmission, refraction, acid and alkali resistance of glass have been carried forward, and glass products such as lens, prism, chemical reaction vessel have been developed. These glass products promoted the revolutionary progress of astronomy, optics, biology and chemistry, and contributed to the birth of modern science. These achievements in science and technology due to glass spread all over the Silk Road. Up to now, astronomical telescopes, microscopes and biochemical experimental equipment are still inseparable from glass components.

In the field of production and living, glass is everywhere. In the field of illumination, building lighting, electronic equipment screens, vehicle portholes, all kinds of special glass are indispensable. It can be said that glass is an important material part of the modern world. As one of the essential human-made materials, glass will continue to walk with the development and progress of human society.

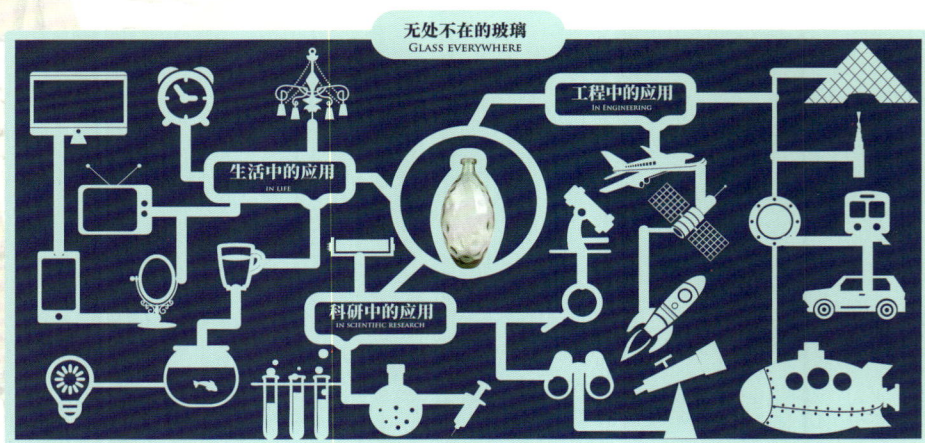

无处不在的玻璃
GLASS EVERYWHERE

生活中的应用 IN LIFE
工程中的应用 IN ENGINEERING
科研中的应用 IN SCIENTIFIC RESEARCH

展项：本展品以艺术化的形态概括了玻璃在现代社会中的广泛应用
Exibit: In an artistic form, this exhibition summarizes the wide application of glass in modern society

3. 古代智慧的新生——蚕丝
The Rebirth of Ancient Wisdom—Silk

　　蚕丝是由熟蚕结茧时所分泌的丝液凝固而成的连续长纤维，早在4700年前中国已利用蚕丝制作了简单的丝织品。现代科技对蚕丝的应用已经远远超出了丝绸纺织领域，以蛋白质为主要成分的蚕丝被开发成各种新型功能性材料。

　　蚕丝经过高分子化学合成处理，使钙或磷与蚕丝凝聚，可开发出骨科治疗上的"蚕丝骨钉"。这种新型"骨钉"比传统上固定断骨的金属钢钉副作用更少，能在体内降解。

　　以蚕丝为原料的丝素膜还可制成"人造皮肤"，以治疗烧伤或其他皮伤。这种"人造皮肤"具有良好的生物相容性，适用于深度烧伤创面的治疗。

　　"蚕丝血管"是由蚕丝纤维、纺织设备和纺织结构形成的螺旋形无缝管状织物。当人体血管病变或受伤时可用相应口径的"蚕丝血管"接上，以挽救人的生命。

Silk is a kind of continuous long fiber which is solidified by the silk liquid secreted by the mature silkworm during cocooning. As early as 4700 years ago, China has made simple silk fabrics from silk. The application of silk in modern science and technology has gone far beyond the field of silk textile. Silk with protein as the main component has been developed into various new functional materials.

Using high molecular chemical synthesis technology, coagulate calcium or phosphorus with silk, creating the "Silk bone nail" for orthopedic treatment. The new "bone nail" has fewer side effects than the traditional metal "steel nail" used to fix broken bones, and can degrade in vivo.

Silk fibroin membrane can also be made into "artificial skin" to treat burn or other skin injuries. This kind of "artificial skin" has good biocompatibility and is suitable for the treatment of deep burn wounds.

Silk vessel is a kind of spiral seamless tubular fabric made by textile equipment with silk fibre. When the human has vascular disease or trauma, the wounded vessels can be connected with the corresponding calibre of silk vessels, to save people's lives.

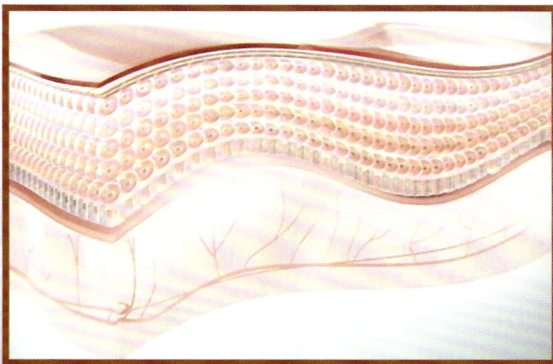

由蚕丝蛋白制成的人造皮肤
Artificial Skin Made of Silk Protein

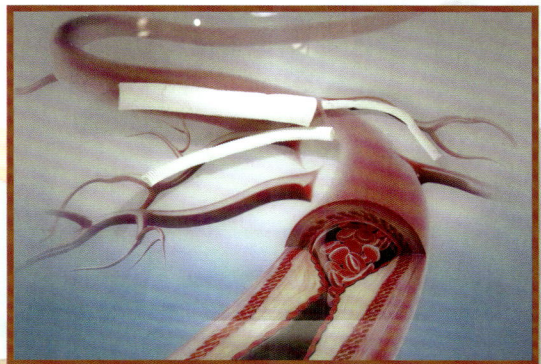

由蚕丝蛋白制成的人造血管
Artificial Skin Made of Silk Protein

4. 古代智慧的新生——陶瓷

The Rebirth of Ancient Wisdom—Ceramics

中国古人运用高超技艺创造了瓷器，在丝绸之路上流传千年。现代科技将古代陶瓷工艺进行信息解码、结构重塑，使器物升华，使陶瓷技术不断焕发出新的活力。

陶瓷耐热、耐蚀、耐磨，并具有潜在的优良的电磁、光学性能。用陶瓷材料制成的传感器可在高温、低温、震动、加速、潮湿、噪声、废气等恶劣条件下使用。

采用隔热性能良好的陶瓷制作的新型涡轮增压发动机能够显著提升汽车发动机的热效率，使燃烧能耗损失降低至52%。

新型陶瓷基复合材料在保持传统陶瓷材料耐高温、高强度、高刚度、密度低、抗腐蚀等优良性能的同时提高了其韧性和可靠性，主要用于航空发动机喷口导流叶片、机翼前缘、涡轮叶片和涡轮罩环等。

除此之外，陶瓷刀具、陶瓷热喷涂技术、陶瓷纤维等新型陶瓷技术正在不断服务于现代生产和生活。

The ancient Chinese used superb skills to create porcelain, which spread on the Silk Road for thousands of years. Modern science and technology decodes the information and remoulds the structure of the ancient ceramic, sublimates the artifacts, stimulating new vitality of ceramics.

Ceramics have heat resistance, corrosion resistance, wear resistance and potential excellent electromagnetic and optical properties. The sensor made of ceramic material can be used in harsh conditions such as extreme temperatures, violent vibration, acceleration, humidity, noise and exhaust gas.

The new turbocharged engine made of ceramic has good thermal insulation performance. This type of engine can significantly improve the thermal efficiency of the automobile engine and reduce the loss of combustion energy consumption to 52%.

The new ceramic matrix composites keep the excellent properties of traditional ceramic materials, such as high temperature resistance, high strength, high stiffness, low density and corrosion resistance, while improving its toughness and reliability. It is mainly used in nozzle guide vane, wing leading edge, turbine blade and turbine cover ring.

In addition, ceramic cutting tools, ceramic thermal spraying technology, ceramic fiber and other new ceramic technologies are continuously of service of modern production and life.

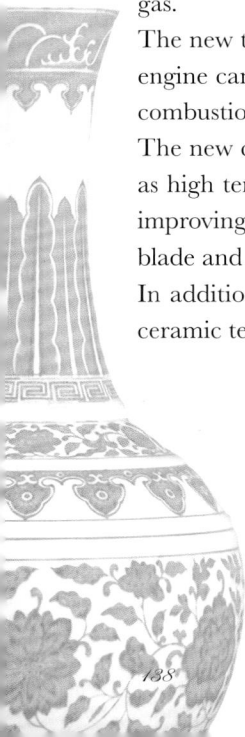

陶瓷纤维
Ceramic fiber

陶瓷热喷涂技术
Ceramic thermal spray coating

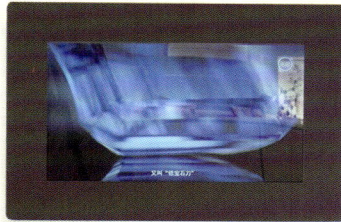

陶瓷发动机
Ceramic automobile engine

陶瓷刀具
Ceramic knives

陶瓷传感器
Ceramic sensor

特种陶瓷
Special Ceramic

5. 古代智慧的新生——信息存取

The Rebirth of Ancient Wisdom—Information Storage and Access

中国古代的织女堪称"编程高手"，她们创造性地发明了"花本技术"。所谓花本就是按照设计好的图案，利用经纬线的上下交叠关系，用线编成一整套花纹记忆存储程序。花本中蕴含着二进制思想：若纬线在经线上（显花），设为"1"；纬线在经线下（不显花），设为"0"；织物呈现为只有"1"和"0"（即显花和不显花）的二进制字符图。利用这种信息存储方式，织女们可以毫不费力地织出花样复杂的图案。

花本式提花机从汉代到宋代不断发展，并经丝绸之路传入西方。19世纪，西方将线制花本改良为穿孔纹板而制成贾卡织机。

20世纪40年代，利用穿孔卡片编程的计算机问世。随后，信息存储媒介层出不穷，信息存取更加高效。中国古代的"花本技术"实现了辉煌的新生。

Woman weavers in ancient China were also "excellent programmers". Via Huaben in the loom, they stored and accessed information on patterns. The word, "Huaben", is a set of pattern memory storage program compiled by threads according to the designed pattern, and using the overlapping relationship of longitude and weft lines as principle. In fact, the Huaben is "binary". When the lateral line is above the longitudinal line (dominant), we set it as "1". When the lateral line is below the longitudinal line (recessive), we set it as "0". The pattern becomes a binary image with only "1" and "0". With this way of information storage, weavers can weave complicated patterns easily.

The Huaben drawloom developed continuously from Han Dynasty to Song Dynasty, and was introduced into the West through the Silk Road. In the 19th century, the jacquard was invented in the West, which improved the Huaben into perforated pattern board.

In the 1940s, the computer with the punch card was invented. Since then, varied information storage media have sprung up. Information storage and retrieval became more efficient. The Huaben technology in ancient China has achieved a brilliant new life.

提花机
Drawloom

②

贾卡织机互动模型：1804年，法国人约瑟夫·贾卡
受花本式提花机启发，做出了首台由踏板控制提花
开口的机械织机，后人称为贾卡织机。其特点是用
提花纹板（穿孔卡片），通过传动机件带动一定顺序
的顶针拉钩，根据花纹组织提升经线而织出花纹
Interaction Model of Jacquard：In 1804, the Frenchman
Joseph jacquard, inspired by the drawloom, made the first
mechanical loom with draw opening controlled by pedals,
which was later called jacquard loom. It is characterized
by using jacquard pattern plate (punch card) to drive a
certain order of thimble hooks through the transmission
mechanism to lift the warp thread according to the pattern
organization and weave the pattern

③

分析机
Analytical Emgine

④

计算机
Computer

6. 信息科技的进化
Evolution of Information Technology

　　文明的历史也是一部信息技术革新演变史。在信息储存方面，古人通过结绳记事首次实现了信息的储存与提取，随后出现了甲骨文、纸张、印刷术、摄影术、打字机等图文载体与复制方式，信息储存的方式和内容量不断扩大。在信息传播方面，古人通过烽火台的光信号首先实现了信息的远距离传输，随着科技的进步，电报、电话、无线电、电视、互联网等技术逐渐普及，信息传播之网覆盖了全世界。今天，伴随技术应用的不断丰富，即时通信、物联网、大数据、云计算、5G、区块链、人工智能、量子通信技术不断涌现，人类正在进入万物互联的信息化、智能化时代。

The history of civilization is also a history of information technology innovation and evolution. In terms of information storage, the ancient people realized the storage and extraction of information for the first time by tying ropes to record events, and then developed image and text carriers and copying methods such as oracle bone inscriptions, paper, printing, photography, typewriters, etc., and the storage mode and internal capacity of information were constantly expanded. In terms of information transmission, the ancients first realized the long-distance transmission of messages through the optical signals of beacon towers. With the progress of science and technology, telegraph, telephone, radio, television, internet and other technologies are gradually popularized, and the network of information dissemination covers the whole world. Today, with the continuous enrichment of technology applications, instant messaging, the internet of things, big data, cloud computing, 5g, blockchain, artificial intelligence, quantum communication technologies are constantly emerging. Human beings are entering the information and intelligent era of Internet of Everything.

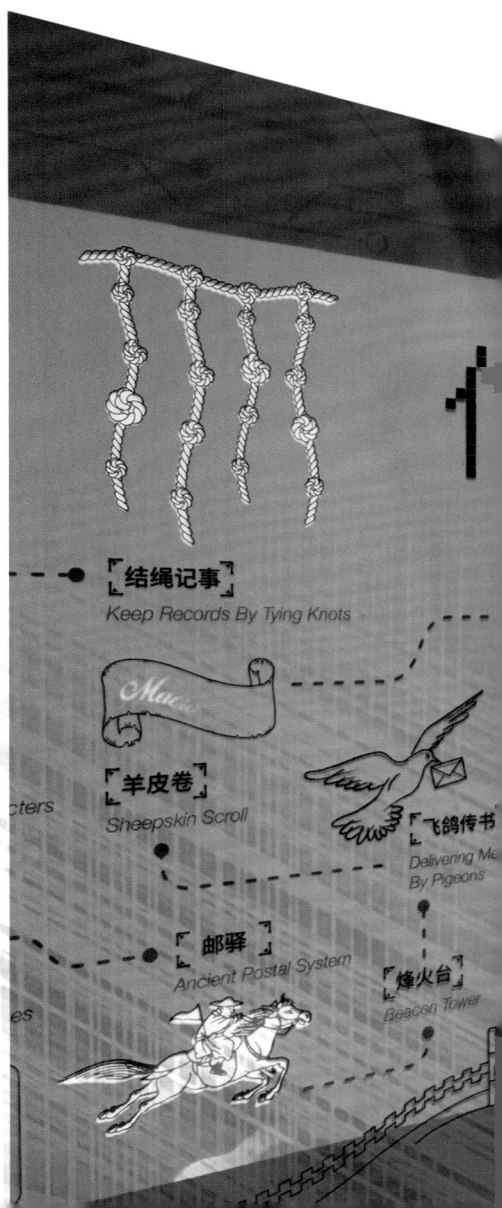

结绳记事
Keep Records By Tying Knots

羊皮卷
Sheepskin Scroll

飞鸽传书
Delivering Ma
By Pigeons

邮驿
Ancient Postal System

烽火台
Beacon Tower

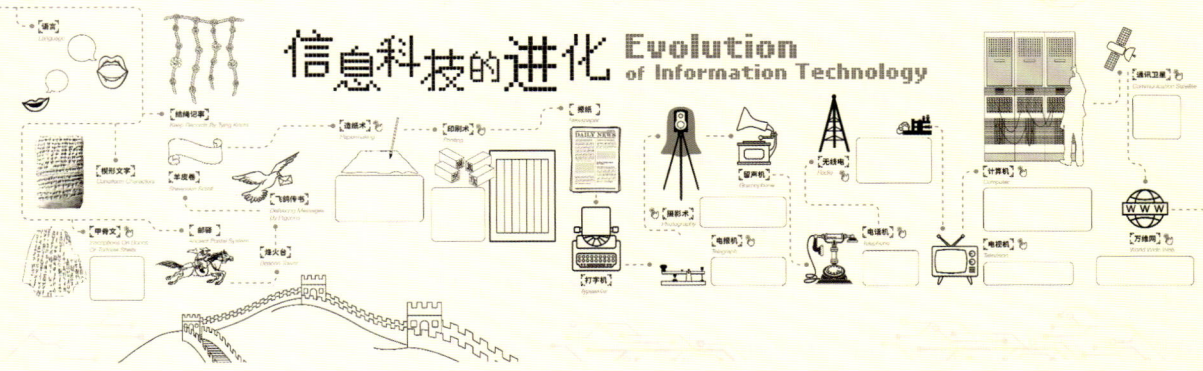

信息科技的进化 Evolution of Information Technology

展项全貌：本展项从人类处理信息的历史中撷取重要科技节点，以动态图解和体感互动的形式，通过不断闪现的动线和变化万端的光影，演示信息技术的进化过程

Full View of Exhibit:This exhibit extracts important technological nodes from the history of human information processing. In the form of dynamic illustration and somatosensory interaction, through constantly flashing moving lines and changing light and shadow, the exhibit demonstrates the development and evolution of information technology

7. "看见"黑洞
"Seeing" Black Hole

从古代伊朗的马拉盖天文台到元代的登封观星台，再到今天的 FAST 射电望远镜，为追求观测的精准，天文仪器不断向大型化发展。但天文仪器的口径不能无限增加，要想获取更加遥远的天体信息，只能依靠国际合作的力量。人类拍摄的首张黑洞照片就是由世界各地的 8 台射电望远镜联网而组成的"事件视界望远镜"所获得的，其等效口径与地球直径相当，其过程体现了"科学无国界"的精神。

From the malagai Observatory in Ancient Iran to Dengfeng Observatory in Yuan Dynasty, and to the FAST radio telescope today, astronomical instruments have been developing to large scale to pursue the accuracy of observation. However, the aperture of astronomical instruments can not be increased indefinitely. To obtain more distant celestial information, the only way is to rely on the power of international cooperation. The first black hole photo taken by human beings was obtained by the event horizon telescope, which was made up of eight radio telescopes all over the world. Its aperture is equivalent to the diameter of the earth. The project of EAST embodied the spirit of "science without borders".

墙象限仪：13世纪，马拉盖天文台建有一座半径大于14英尺（约4.27米）的墙象限仪。古代伊朗天文学家认为仪器尺寸越大，测量的精度则越高，这种理念也影响到中国天文仪器的研制

Wall Gauge : In the 13th century, the Maragha Observatory had a wall gauge with a radius of more than 14 feet.Islamic astronomers believed that the larger the instrument size,

登封观象台：建于13世纪，相当于一座大型圭表，其高度是传统表高的5倍，影子长度也长了5倍，测量误差减小为传统圭表的1/5

Dengfeng Observatory : Equivalent to a large-scale gnomon-and-ruler, built in the 13th century, its height is five times higher than that of the traditional one, and the shadow length is also five times longer. The measurement error is reduced to one fifth of that of the traditional

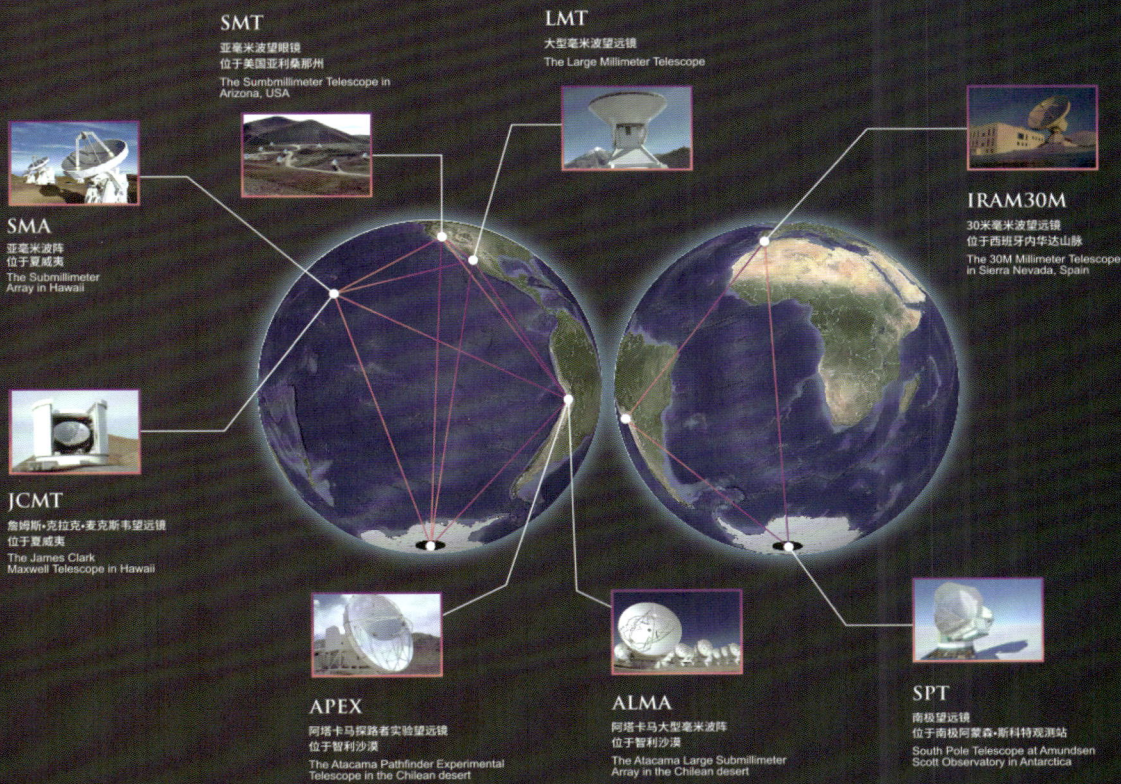

SMT
亚毫米波望眼镜
位于美国亚利桑那州
The Sumbmillimeter Telescope in
Arizona, USA

LMT
大型毫米波望远镜
The Large Millimeter Telescope

IRAM30M
30米毫米波望远镜
位于西班牙内华达山脉
The 30M Millimeter Telescope
in Sierra Nevada, Spain

SMA
亚毫米波阵
位于夏威夷
The Submillimeter
Array in Hawaii

JCMT
詹姆斯·克拉克·麦克斯韦望远镜
位于夏威夷
The James Clark
Maxwell Telescope in Hawaii

APEX
阿塔卡马探路者实验望远镜
位于智利沙漠
The Atacama Pathfinder Experimental
Telescope in the Chilean desert

ALMA
阿塔卡马大型毫米波阵
位于智利沙漠
The Atacama Large Submillimeter
Array in the Chilean desert

SPT
南极望远镜
位于南极阿蒙森·斯科特观测站
South Pole Telescope at Amundsen
Scott Observatory in Antarctica

事件视界望远镜地理分布图
Geographical Distribution of Event Horizon Telescopes

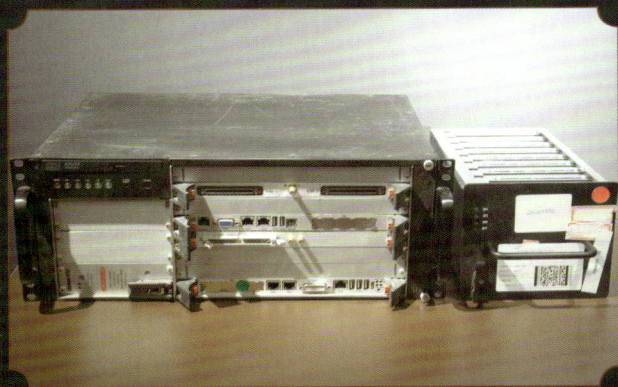

中国科学院上海天文台参与黑洞成像的电脑机箱与硬盘阵列
Computer Case and Hard Disk Array for Black Hole Imaging at Shanghai
Observatory, Chinese Academy of Sciences

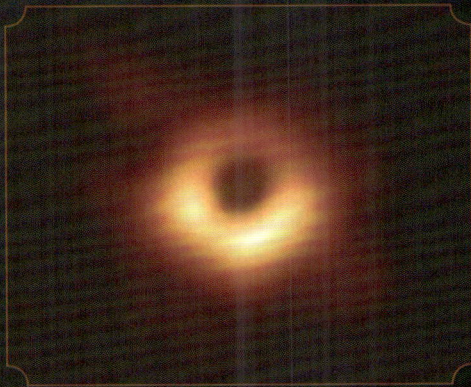

首张黑洞照片
First Photo of Black Hole

8. 守望丝路的卫星
The Satellite Watching the Silk Road

　　各种应用卫星为"一带一路"的互联互通提供可靠保障。北斗导航卫星可在全球范围内提供高精度定位与授时服务，目前已服务近30个"一带一路"沿线国家。"风云"气象卫星系列为气象、海洋、农业等领域提供数据服务，目前正在为47个"一带一路"国家提供气象数据。此外，中国的通信卫星系统、资源卫星系统也在为"一带一路"建设提供重要的科技支撑。

All kinds of application satellites provide a reliable guarantee for interconnection of the Belt and Road Initiative. Beidou navigation satellite can provide high-precision positioning and timing services in the global range. At present, it has served nearly 30 countries along the Belt and Road. The "Fengyun" meteorological satellite series provides data services for meteorological, marine, agricultural and other fields, and is currently giving meteorological data to 47 countries. Besides, China's communication satellite system and resource satellite system are also providing necessary scientific and technological support for the Belt and Road construction.

"北斗三号"导航卫星系统：由位于中圆轨道、地球静止轨道、倾斜地球同步轨道的30颗卫星构成
"Beidou-3" Navigation Satellite System : Composed of 30 satellites located in mid circle orbit, geostationary orbit and inclined geostationary orbit

"风云三号"气象卫星：越过南、北极的极地轨道卫星
"FengYun-3" Meteorological Satellite : A polar orbiting satellite crossing the Antarctic and Arctic

高分卫星系统：由地球静止轨道和低轨道卫星组成
The High Resolution Satellite System : Consists of geostationary orbit and low orbit satellites

"海洋二号"卫星运行在太阳同步轨道上
"Haiyang-2" Satellite Is In the Sun Synchronous Orbit

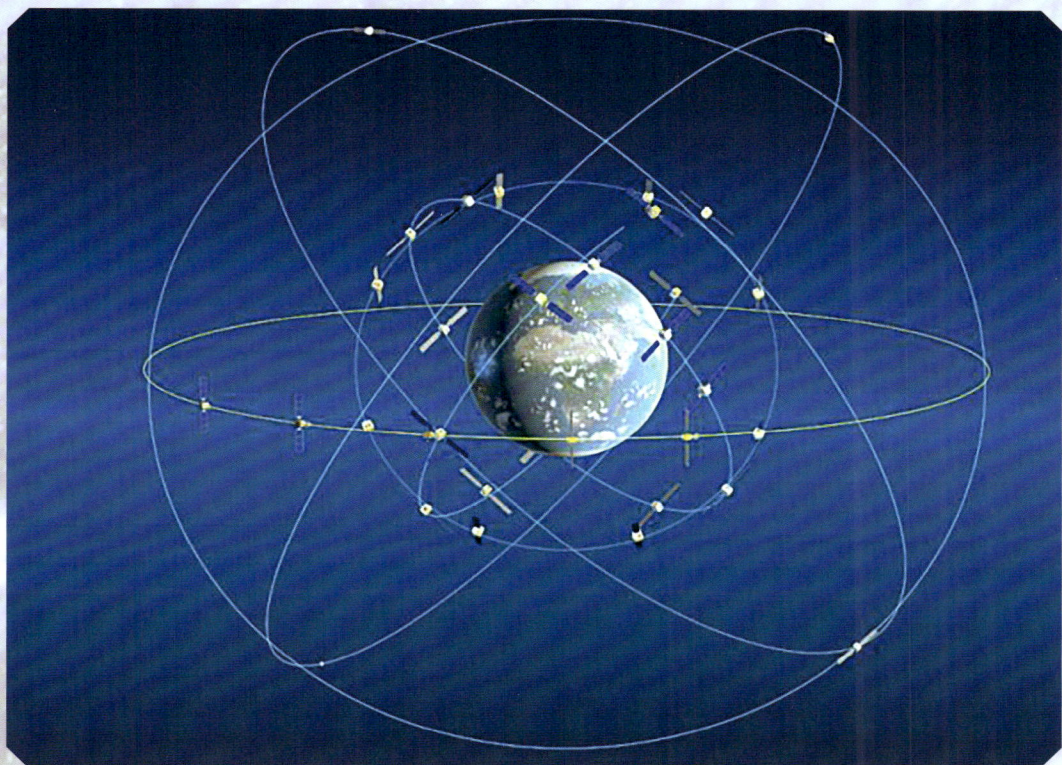

"北斗三号"导航卫星（上）
"Beidou-3" Navigation Satellite（Top）

"风云三号"气象卫星（中左）
"FengYun-3" Meteorological Satellite（Middle Left）

高分卫星（中右）
High Resolution Satellite（Middle Right）

"海洋二号"卫星（下）
"Haiyang-2" Satellite（Bottom）

9. 世界变小了
The World Is Getting Smaller

　　交通工具的速度影响着人类文明的进程，每一次交通技术的进步都推动着文明的交流与发展。交错纵横的道路、姿态各异的桥梁、功能多样的马车、各具特色的船舶……它们呈现着古代交通的风采，缩短了人与人的距离。

　　现代社会，交通基础设施不断完善，交通工具先进，交通以前所未有的力量改变着生活与生产方式。港珠澳大桥由桥梁、隧道和人工岛组成，创下多项"世界之最"；智能码头将集装箱由自动化轨道桥吊装至无人驾驶电动卡车，作业过程如行云流水；空中交通拉近了各大洲之间的距离；"智能高铁""绿色高铁"使世界紧密相连；盾构机打通了地下空间。

　　在新的丝绸之路上，"中国制造"促进了海、陆、空交通的蓬勃发展，不仅提升了社会运行效率，更为国际经济文化交流贡献力量。交通工具的革新拉近了各国之间的距离，让世界不断变"小"。

The speed of transportation affects the process of human civilization, and every progress of transportation technology promotes the communication and development of civilization. Crisscross roads, bridges with different forms, carriages with various functions, ships with different characteristics... they have presented the elegant demeanor of ancient traffic and shortened the distance between people and the world.

In the modern society, with the continuous improvement of the infrastructure and the means of transportation, transportation is changing the way of people's life and production with unprecedented force. The Zhuhai Hong Kong Macao Bridge is composed of bridges, tunnels and artificial islands, has broken many world records; intelligent wharf lift containers from automated rail bridges to driverless electric trucks with smooth operation process; air traffic shortens the distance between continents.; intelligent high-speed rail and Green high-speed rail connect the world closely; shield machines connect underground spaces.

On the new Silk Road, "made in China" has promoted the vigorous development of sea, land and air transportation, not only improving the efficiency of social operation, but also contributing to international economic and cultural exchanges. The innovation of means of transportation is bridgjing distant countries and making the world smaller and smaller.

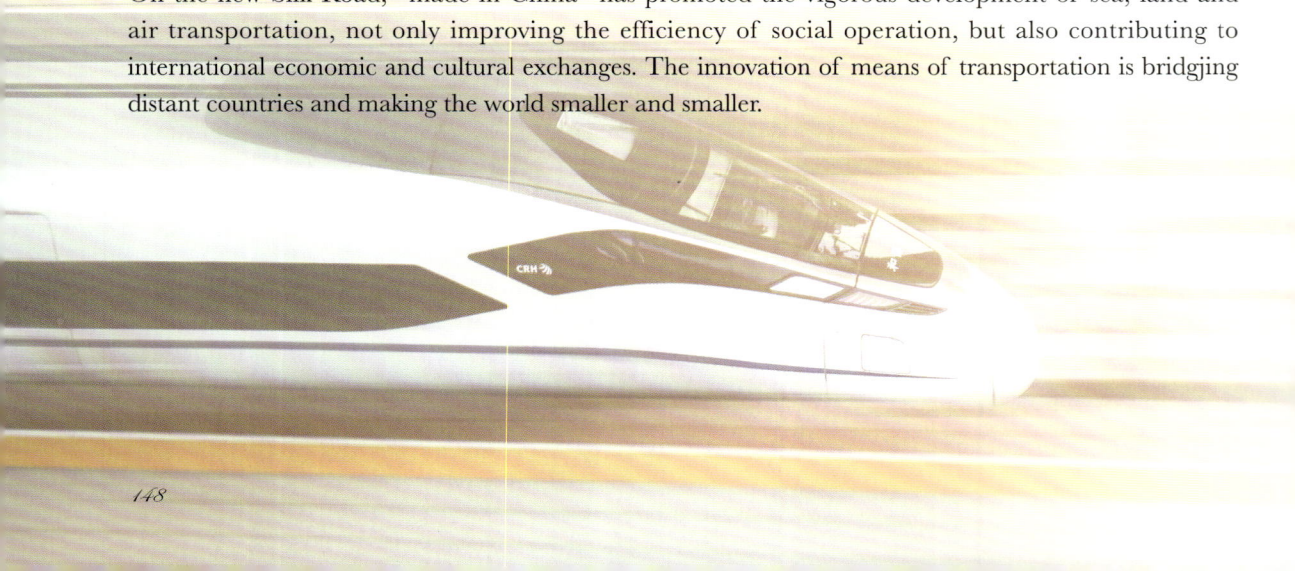

陇海铁路铁轨实物（1913年汉阳铁厂制造）和京张高铁无砟轨道实物（2019年中铁十四局制造）
The Track of Longhai Railway (Manufactured by Hanyang Iron Works in 1913) and the Ballastless Track of Beijing Zhang High Speed Railway (Manufactured by China Railway 14th Bureau in 2019)

盾构机模型
Model of Shield Machine

交通领域的"中国制造"：C919民用客机、"复兴号"高铁、盾构机、集装箱滚装船
"Made in China" in Transportation Field: C919 civil airliner, "Fuxing" high speed railway, shield machine, container roll-on-roll-off ship

10. 共绘 21 世纪丝绸之路
Drawing the Silk Road in the 21st Century

在科技、信息、交通、文化高度发达的21世纪，每一个普通人都是各类交往中最活跃、最核心的元素，也必将在"一带一路"建设中扮演越来越重要的角色。每个人都可以畅想、探索自己的"丝绸之路"，人人都可以成为新时代的"马可·波罗"。在本展项中，观众通过趣味答题的形式回顾展览各单元的体验与知识，系统会根据观众的观展情况为其定制个性化的"丝绸之路"，体验结束后，观众的头像会出现在投影的世界地图上，沿着属于观众个人的"丝绸之路"进行探索。在这里，千千万万的观众将共创21世纪新丝绸之路，成为促进东西方科技与文化交流的新使者。

In the 21st century, when science and technology, information, transportation and culture are highly developed, every ordinary person is the most active and core element in all kinds of communications. Every ordinary person will play an increasingly important role in the "One Belt One Road" construction. Everyone can imagine and explore their own "Silk Road" and become "Marco Polo" in the new era. In this exhibit, the visitors will review the experience and knowledge of each unit of the exhibition in the form of answering interesting questions. The system will customize the personalized "Silk Road" according to the audience's answers, then, the head image of the visitors will appear on the projected world map and explore along audience personal "Silk Road". Here, tens of thousands of visitors will jointly create a new Silk Road in the 21st century and become a new messenger to promote the exchange of science and technology and culture between the East and the West.

观众头像沿着新"丝路"探索
The Visitors'Portrait Explore along the New "Silk Road"

观众进行多媒体互动操作
The Visitors Interactive with the Multimedia Software

Messages From Tu Youyou

时代在发展，科技在创新，社会在进步，人类命运共同体需要我们为之共同努力。我可以想象你们充满了朝气和活力，我更深信你们肩负着人类的未来和希望。我衷心期待年轻的一代能勇于担当、能栋梁辈出、能超越前人，你们一定能为人类创造一个更加美好的明天。

Along with the developing times, our society is progressing with innovating science and technology. To build a community with a shared future for mankind requires all of us to work together. I could imagine that you are full of vigor and vitality. I am even more convinced that you would carry the future and hope for mankind. And I sincerely hope that the younger generation will be brave enough to take responsibility, be able to come forth in large numbers, and surpass their predecessors. You would definitely create a better tomorrow for mankind.

屠呦呦

2019年12月

图书在版编目（CIP）数据

做一天马可·波罗：发现丝绸之路的智慧：汉英对照 / 赵洋主编 . —北京：北京科学技术出版社，2021.9

ISBN 978－7－5714－1687－4

Ⅰ . ①做… Ⅱ . ①赵… Ⅲ . ①丝绸之路—通俗读物—汉、英 Ⅳ . ① K 928.6－49

中国版本图书馆 CIP 数据核字 (2021) 第 143081 号

策划编辑：许苏葵
责任编辑：许苏葵
责任印制：吕　越
封面设计：刘林子
版式设计：北京麦莫瑞文化传播有限公司
出 版 人：曾庆宇
出版发行：北京科学技术出版社
社　　址：北京西直门南大街 16 号
邮政编码：100035
电　　话：0086－10－66135495（总编室）
　　　　　0086－10－66113227（发行部）
网　　址：www.bkydw.cn
印　　刷：北京博海升彩色印刷有限公司
开　　本：710 mm × 1000 mm 1/16
字　　数：20.5 千字
印　　张：9.75
版　　次：2021 年 9 月第 1 版
印　　次：2021 年 9 月第 1 次印刷
ISBN　978－7－5714－1687－4

定　价：98.00 元